Euripides' *Medea*
The Incarnation of Disorder

Euripides' *Medea*
The Incarnation of Disorder

Emily A. McDermott

The Pennsylvania State University Press
University Park and London

Library of Congress Cataloging-in-Publication Data

McDermott, Emily A.
Euripides' *Medea*.

Bibliography: p.
Includes index.
1. Euripides. Medea. 2. Medea (Greek mythology)
in literature. 3. Order in literature. 1. Title.
PA3973.M4M38 1989   882'.01   88-17905
ISBN 0-271-00647-1

τοῖς τε θρέψασι
τῷτε συμπαιδοτροφοῦντι

Contents

Acknowledgments

I owe thanks to many people for their assistance and support in the preparation of this study: to Richard Hamilton and Ava Chitwood, for their readings of early versions of the manuscript; to the publisher's two readers, Bernard M. W. Knox and Robert D. Lamberton, for many clarifying comments; to Frank J. Nisetich, for his reading and for advice on the translations from the Greek; to Robert A. Corrigan, for giving me the summer I needed to finish the manuscript; to Richard B. Sewall, for his reading, his encouragement, and his generous help; to C. F. Ahern, for frequent technological consultation; to my colleague and friend R. J. Schork, *grande columen rerum*, who worked his way through more versions than either of us likes to remember; and, most of all, to my husband, Richard Sewall, and my children, Ethan, Alexandra, Eric, and Michaela—who forbore.

Except as otherwise noted, the text cited is the Oxford Classical Text edited by Gilbert Murray. I have included translations of Greek quotations and a glossary of Greek terms and names in order to make the study available to as broad an audience as possible. With only a few noted exceptions, translations are my own; I have tried to keep them faithful to the sense of the original without indulging any inchoate poetic inclinations. Abbreviations and transliterations of Greek names appear as they are found in the *Oxford Classical Dictionary*[2].

Introduction

Aside from the pro-satyric *Alcestis* of 438 B.C., the *Medea* is the first of
Euripides' tragedies passed down to us. It was produced in the year
that the Peloponnesian War began. It presents us with the first in a
parade of vivid female tragic protagonists across the Euripidean stage.
Awarded last prize by the Athenian judges who witnessed its premier
offering, and recurrently decried as flawed by form- or logic-conscious
critics, it has nevertheless won accolades from the fourth century B.C.
on throughout the centuries as one of the most powerful of the Greek
tragedies.

Turbulence in assessment of the play issues from and centers on the
character of Medea herself. Simply put, the quandary is this: what to do
with a tragic protagonist who is at once heroic, sympathetic, and morally repugnant. Medea, as protagonist, is clearly majestic: she is emphatically cast by the playwright in the mold of the tragic hero;[1] the
power of her wrath and will inspires admiration and awe. As an outcast, she further draws from the audience (as from the Chorus) an
instinctive sympathy. Yet her actions in the course of the play range
from deceitful to utterly repellent. On the other hand, Jason has descended, in Euripides' hands, to a nonhero. The playwright has taken
none of the steps which might have rendered him a grand-scale oppo-
nent for Medea. In defending his actions against Medea, Jason invokes
no opposite principle (as Sophocles' Creon does against Antigone, for

example, or as Aeschylus's Clytemnestra does against Agamemnon), but only a specious pragmatism. Jason's is the fall of the mediocre man. Not even the piteousness of his ruin can raise him to the ranks of tragic hero or make him a truly sympathetic character.

The confusion of sympathies and moral judgment aroused by the collocation of these two dramatic characters is emblematic of the confusion perennially experienced by those who would assess and explain Euripides the playwright. What is he ultimately saying to us? Euripidean critics have asked that question and its corollary (*What does he believe?*) many times, and in many contexts. The diversity of their responses is chaotic and, at the same time, illuminating; a multitude of categorizations, often antithetical, have been invoked in the attempt to circumscribe Euripides' art. Knox has aptly characterized the problem, noting only some of the "-ism's" attributed to Euripides: ". . . the field is wide open for every man to make his own Euripides—the rationalist, the irrationalist, the political dramatist, the philosopher, the feminist, the radical, the reactionary, or the mere bungler."[2]

All such categorizations, however, no matter how much of truth they may contain, must fall short in the end, for it is in the very nature of Euripides' art to decline to answer these quintessential (and legitimately posed) questions of audience to playwright (*What are you telling us? What do you believe?*). In a recent essay, Knox has further noted "the discords [Euripides'] plays inflict on our ears" and has concluded: "He must have intended to produce this unsettling effect, which disturbed his contemporaries as it disturbs us: to leave us with a sense of uncertainty, painfully conscious now, if not before, of the treacherous instability of the world in which we live, its utter unpredictability, its intractability. It might be said of him what the Corinthians in Thucydides say of the Athenians, that he was born never to live in peace himself and to prevent the rest of mankind from doing so."[3] Later in the essay, Knox further asserts: "In Euripidean tragedy old certainties are shattered; what seems solid cracks and melts, foundations are torn up, direction lost."[4] These two comments by a sensitive and insightful critic support and complement the view of Euripidean artistry from which this exposition of the *Medea* arises: that it portrays a world from which all order has been pointedly removed, and the very reality or even potentiality of order is implicitly denied. Euripides' plays invert, subvert, and pervert traditional assertions of order; they challenge their audience's most basic tenets and assumptions about the moral, social, and civic fabric of mankind and replace them with nothing; that is, while the playwright seeks to uproot mental complacencies, he will not move to substitute for them a new vision based on clearly articulated values of his own.

Euripides' art may thus be said to have a nihilistic effect. To make such an assertion is not to append yet another "-ist" (and one so potentially unpopular) to the catalogue of epithets bestowed on the playwright by critics. Perhaps it will seem too fine a distinction to decline to apply the term "nihilist" to Euripides himself, as if he were a professor of a particular school of philosophy or an ideologue espousing a specific party doctrine, and yet to speak of his plays' nihilistic effect. Nevertheless, there is a real distinction between the two, for Euripides does not preach the senselessness of life and personally may not even have believed in it; his plays merely tend to suggest it, as he is seemingly compelled, through his characters' utterances, actions, and afflictions, to set up truths only to question their reality, to contradict them, or efface them. In a recent study of Euripides, Pietro Pucci compares himself, as critic, to Penelope, simultaneously weaving and unweaving the threads of his argument; the same comparison is implicitly made to apply to Euripides.[5] This simile is a fitting characterization of a playwright who so often sets about weaving a dramatic tapestry apparently recognizable in its assumptions and its traditions—then rapidly unravels it, before his audience's eyes, and to their utmost befuddlement and consternation.

This study will explicate aspects of a single play, the *Medea*, as conducive of an overarching sense of disorder. Critics have often noted a clear correlation between the chronological progress (or, rather, deterioration) of the Peloponnesian War and a growing element of bitterness within Euripides' extant plays. In fact, presented with what one critic has described as the "howling spiritual lunacy" of the *Orestes* of 408 B.C.,[6] probably very few would rear indignantly at the very breath of the word "nihilism." However, the patent extremism of the *Orestes* makes it possible to approach that late play as an exceptional case and so to salvage Euripides' artistic soul from the "taint" of an unredeeming negativism. This study, however, will assert that a shocking challenge to presumptions of order is also at the heart of the first of Euripides' tragedies passed down to us, written before the actual onset of war, and that this challenge in fact constitutes an abiding principle of Euripides' artistry. For while this study will confine itself to elucidation of the *Medea*, the poetic techniques identified here are not limited to one play. The *Medea* is clearly an outstanding *exemplum*, in that the protagonist's actions partake supremely of contempt for the normal postulates and prescripts of hu-

man life. Both the techniques by which the playwright produces a
disordered dramatic world and that world's disconcerting effect on
his audiences, however, are common to much of his corpus. In a
sense, then, the *Medea* may be taken as paradigmatic.

A primary critical approach to Euripides adopted in this study rests
on the fundamental tenet that one who seeks for meaning in Euripides' tragedies will come closest to finding it by examining everything
in the play (characters, their actions, choruses, mythic plots and allusions to myth, place within literary traditions, and use of conventions) in close conjunction with a feasible reconstruction of the audience's expectations in each regard, for it is a keynote of Euripides'
dramaturgy to resist an easy or predictable fulfillment of those expectations, and indeed to challenge the moral and social norms and the
dramatic conventions which form their basic underpinnings. Corollary to this frustration of expectation is the playwright's penchant for
the anomaly, which has perennially irritated critics,[7] but which can
readily be seen to serve his dual purpose of surprising his audience
and of challenging their conceptual premises. Robert Eisner begins an
article on Euripides' use of myth with a telling epigraph from Nabokov: "Competition in chess problems is not really between White and
Black but between the composer and the hypothetical solver (just as
in a first-rate work of fiction the real clash is not between the characters but between the author and the world)."[8] Euripides' game is to
create his effects, both major and minor, by frustrating his audience,
startling them, and finally leaving them groping, Orpheus-like, after a
receding articulation of meaning.

Almost every critic of Euripides, of course, has on some occasion
noted particular instances of Euripidean twists and surprises. Of those
fewer who have systematically examined the achievement of the unexpected as a principle of Euripidean artistry, I shall cite here only a
minimal representative sample. Burnett's examination of typologies of
plot and scene and her analysis of the effects of Euripides' aberration
from their conventions have been seminal.[9] Knox has elucidated in
many places and with an inevitably sure touch different aspects of
Euripides' art of "deformation."[10] Eisner explicates Euripides' use of
myth in terms of the recurrent anomaly caused by the juxtaposition of
qualitatively different realities.[11] Hamilton has pointed out subtle com-
plications even in that aspect of Euripides' plays where he is most often
viewed as depriving the play of suspense: the predictive prologue.[12]
Winnington-Ingram, Arnott, and Nisetich have retailed examples of
the playwright's self-conscious manipulation of stage conventions.[13] A

recent study by Newton of the allusion to Ino at lines 1282–84 of the play, in analyzing both the substantive anomaly of the equation between Ino and Medea there suggested by the Chorus and the significant variation made by Euripides in the normal mode of argumentation by mythological *exemplum*, itself becomes (though it is brief and specifically delimited) paradigmatic of the type of critical examination into Euripides' art of deformation that I am describing.[14] Buttrey's exegesis of the *Medea* is the first of which I am aware to have systematically studied the play from the perspective of audience expectation.[15]

If one takes Euripides' propensity for deformations as a fundamental principle of his art and, essentially, as a purpose in itself, many of the classic problems in Euripidean criticism disappear or are at least alleviated. If Euripides aims at anomaly, uncertainty, and confusion, then when he achieves it we need not assume dramatic flaws or authorial failure to make himself clear—because he did not set out to clarify in the first place. There is, necessarily, a facile element in this line of reasoning, and one must be watchful. "Euripides has created confusion; therefore it is Euripides' purpose to create confusion." *Caveat criticus:* used indiscriminately, the argument could lead to its own brand of chaos. But used discreetly and based on prudent examination of the evidence provided by the text and other pertinent sources, it is illuminating.

The present study proceeds from the premise that Medea's murder of her children is the key to Euripides' play, both dramatically and thematically. Taking the love of mother for child as normative of cosmic order, as the effective *sine qua non* of human morality, the playwright turns Medea's violent breach of this order to such devastating dramatic use that in the end not only the character Medea but the play itself has become an embodiment of disorder.

A major question in Euripidean scholarship has been whether Euripides was the first to introduce the deliberate child-murder into the Medea-saga. The first chapter of this study will review the primary sources on which this debate rests and join the scholarly discourse on the issue by both evaluating previous secondary literature on the subject and presenting a reading of two passages within the *Medea* which may provide internal evidence that in having Medea kill her sons to gain vengeance on their father Euripides is forging new mythic ground. Nonetheless, in recognition that the paucity and ambiguity of the available evidence concerning innovation will continue to preclude sure resolution of this question, the stance to be adopted in this study is twofold: that the evidence leads fairly to a judgment that the motif of Medea's purposeful violence against her children was Euripides' innovation into the saga; but that, even if one assumes that his original audience knew in advance of the deliberate child-murder as a mythic option available to Euripides, the artistry of his play may be seen to be emphatically concentrated on the creation of agonizing suspense concerning the precise nature of the fate he will mete out to the children at the end of the play.

The second chapter discusses the techniques by which Euripides leads his audience to the realization that, in his version of mythic events, Medea's children will not die by accident or mischance (as they do in some sources), nor at the hands of the angry Corinthians (as they do in others), but by Medea's own purposeful hand. The playwright uses consummate artistry to pull the audience's emotions and expectations alternately this way and that and to maximize the suspense and eventual revulsion that will afflict the audience as they come to understand the mother's abhorrent intent.

In the past several decades, a handful of critics have undertaken parallel analyses of this process of revelation. Buttrey argues that the initial Athenian audience would not have registered at all on what those who know in advance of the child-murder see as foreshadowings, except to foresee harm to the children from the Corinthians and to reflect pityingly on the irony of Medea's ignorance of it.[16] This view—while it offers an important corrective to failure to appreciate the surprise element in Medea's revelation—does not fully recognize the turbulence of audience expectation perpetrated by Euripides throughout the first half of the play. Easterling and Bongie chart a middle course, noting the prologue's emphatic foreshadowing of harm to the children while still allowing a certain element of surprise to Medea's revelation of the form her revenge will take.[17] The critic who has come closest to the view to be presented here of an alternate planting of true but ambiguous foreshadowings and deliberately misleading clues, for the purpose of heightened suspense, is Elliott, in a school edition of the play.[18] For the sake of fluency of argument and cohesion of the general thesis of this study, I have undertaken to present a step-by-step explication of the revelation and its effects, rather than merely to note areas of agreement and disagreement with these and other earlier commentators; certain of the specific points made here, however, have been noted by previous critics.

The impact of Euripides' virtuosity in leading up to Medea's revelation is forceful: the audience cannot but feel the utter centrality to the play of Medea's climactic crime.[19] They cannot but wonder what the playwright intends by presenting us with a dramatic world in which such a character may dwell.

The third chapter will examine the complex question of Medea as woman. The very plot of the *Medea*, which is centered on the response of a wife to her husband's defection and betrayal of his pledged fidelity, makes it all but inevitable that the play's themes will include the classic opposition of Man and Woman. Euripides has chosen to underline emphatically the thematic importance of this conflict through numerous explicit statements placed in the mouths of his characters. One of Medea's first onstage concerns is to provide an affecting and polemical picture of the unenviable helplessness of women in Greek society (see lines 230ff., quoted below, pp. 45–46). The Chorus sings hopefully of the reversal in repute to come for much-slandered Woman (lines 410ff.). By contrast, not only Jason (see especially lines 569–75) but the female Chorus (see lines 1290–92) and even Medea (at lines 407–9) utter misogynistic tags in the tradition of Hesiod, Semonides, and others. Despite these explicit signals, critics have often shied away from the notion that the play speaks of male/female conflicts in their universality or that the Athenian audience was meant to see in Medea (the foreign "witch") a threat to their own social order. Recent criticism, however, has pointed decisively in the other direction, leading to the recognition that the conflict of Jason and Medea—husband and wife, father and mother of the same children—culminating in the woman's unspeakable breach of her societally appointed role as wife and mother, must necessarily have made an adverse comment on fifth-century Athenian mores and struck chords of disquiet in the Athenian audience.[20] This study will continue the discourse concerning Euripides' approach in this play to the conflict between men and women. Specific attention will be given to the eventual effect of Medea's early identification of herself with Everywoman; to the "wavering scene," in which Medea carries on an interior dialogue, alternately faltering and resteeling herself to her resolve to slay her sons; and to aspects of the Chorus's reactions to Medea as reflective of "normal" human sensibility.

The fourth chapter continues to treat the play's concern with the conflict between men and women, but from the particular vantage point of literary convention. Attention will be directed here to Euripides' inveterate overturn of audience expectation: as the play progresses, the playwright belies his own early suggestions that this play's thematic handling of the classic conflict between Male and Female will fall within a literary tradition exemplified by Aeschylus's

Oresteia and Sophocles' *Antigone*. Through the resultant dislocation of this play from earlier tragic treatments of the universality and metaphysical significance of the conflict between the sexes, the author has underscored the essential nihilism of the play, for in its end the Male/Female conflict is proved meaningless, as both sexes (as represented by Jason and Medea) are indicted and convicted of betrayal of the most basic human responsibilities and values.

The final two chapters turn to detailed explication of the centrality to the play of the theme of *trophē:* "nurture." In the Greek conception, the proper functioning of both social and civic orders may be comprehended by the reciprocally enjoined requirements of *trophē.* The social order is maintained by strict adherence within the family to the rule that parents and children reciprocally nurture one another in their respective ages of helplessness. Likewise, the civic order is supported by the assumption of a mutuality of nurture between citizen and state. Chapters 5 and 6 elucidate the many appearances of the theme of *trophē*, both familial and civic, in the Medea-saga as Euripides presents it. It is perhaps through the heroine's repeated assaults on this fundamental and sacred value that the playwright most persuasively portrays her as an incarnation of disorder. And, as so often, the sense of disarray perpetrated by the characters' movements is compounded by the play's very technique, for throughout his treatment of the theme of *trophē,* and most specifically in his use and abuse of the characters of the two fathers and kings, Creon and Aegeus, Euripides questions the conventional, brings about the unexpected, and ultimately leaves his audience foundationless.

1

Medea *Teknophonos:*
The Sources

I

Ask any casual reader of literature who the mythic character Medea was, and what she did, and, if they have any answer at all, it will almost certainly be that she killed her children. And with good reason: the murder of the children is clearly the central fact—the crux—of Euripides' play; and Euripides' play is, in turn, the canonical literary source for the Corinthian exploits and the general character of Medea. Beside the play's grotesque finale, Medea's previous murders of the princess and her father, Creon—as graphically detailed as they are—become almost incidental. Beside it, the quibbling and recriminations of husband and wife are mere pettiness. Medea is a mother who will kill the children she loves, simply to devastate the husband she hates.

Because the child-murder stands so firmly in our minds as both Medea's ultimate act and her ultimate characterizing element, it comes as something of a shock to those tutored in the Greek dramatists' relation to the realm of received myth to find that this crime may not have been a traditional element in the Medea-saga, but Euripides' own invention. The mythic evidence, as so often, is scanty, but two major pre-Euripidean variants concerning the children's fate are partially attested. In one, they apparently died accidentally when Medea tried to effect their immortality; in this version Jason and Medea jointly form the ruling house of Corinth, the kingship having passed to Jason on a matrilocal principle from Medea's father, Aeetes. According to the second tradition, however, Medea's children were killed by the Corinthians, in revenge for Medea's murder of their king (the motive for his murder is not stated); the Corinthians subsequently spread the slanderous rumor that Medea herself had caused the children's death. There is no extant pre-Euripidean source which indicts the sorceress for the willful and unnatural murder of her children.

The question, then, naturally presents itself to the critic whether Medea's deliberate murder of her sons was an innovation into the myth made by Euripides himself. Such innovations are certainly characteristic of his art, on both the large and the small scale.[1] Remarkable gains would be made in critical insight into the play and the playwright if this question could be answered definitively, for any alterations and innovations made by a classical author into the traditions, and especially an alteration as radical as this one, become handles through which the critic may help to open the inner chambers of the poet's mind and artistic design. Unfortunately, the ever-troubled task of reconstruction of classical sources, both mythic and literary, is no less difficult in this case than in others. The evidence is as deftly elusive as Proteus. However, the critical gains to be made even by a nondefinitive examination into this central question are significant if we, like Odysseus, persevere.

II

Let us look again and in more detail at the mythic sources.[2] The tradition by which Medea, as rightful queen of Corinth, inadvertently causes her children's death (the *phonos akousios:* "involuntary killing" motif) stems from Eumelus (a Corinthian of the seventh century B.C.); it is attested in the Scholia to Pindar (*Olympian* 13.74) and in Pausanias (2.3.10–11). The tradition that the children were killed by Corinthian citizens avenging the death of their king stems from Creophylus, as paraphrased by the Alexandrian commentator Didymus (see Schol. *Med.* 264). A version attributed to another Alexandrian, Parmeniscus, by the same scholiast in a sense mediates between these two traditions: it joins Creophylus in attributing the murder of Medea's children to the Corinthians (though only to the women, in Parmeniscus's version), but the murder is motivated by their rebellion against rule by a foreign sorceress and so depends on the ancestral link between Corinth and Colchis cited by Eumelus.

Presented with this reconstructed mythic evidence, critics have adopted stances which Séchan has described as falling into three broad categories, those, respectively, of "l'originalité absolue," "l'originalité relative," and "l'originalité réduite." The first, espoused by Wilamowitz, is the most extreme, since it involves both denial of Euripides' familiarity with the *phonos akousios* motif (as in Eumelus) and disbelief in the early existence of a tradition that the murder had been slanderously attributed to Medea (as attested by Didymus); it has also been taken to run counter to a passage in Aristotle's *Poetics* (14.1453ᵇ.27–29).³ The view of "l'originalité absolue" has accordingly fallen into some desuetude. In this century, the struggle has been primarily between proponents of the second and third views identified by Séchan. The intermediate stance (that of "l'originalité relative") is well exemplified by Page, whose summary of the mythic evidence is as follows: "It is now clear that Euripides knew two stories which might suggest to him his innovation. In Eumelos, Medea killed her children accidentally; in Kreophylos, Medea was falsely rumored to have killed her children deliberately."⁴ Page thus concludes (in agreement with numerous predecessors) that the deliberate child-murder was not a known mythic variant before the' fifth century and that it was Euripides in his *Medea* (and not the shadowy Neophron) who introduced this innovation into the saga by transforming an involuntary (and well-intentioned) killing into premeditated vengeance against an unfaithful husband. He is followed in both inferences by the majority of subsequent scholars.⁵

On the other hand, the school of "l'originalité réduite" is persuaded that the tradition of the voluntary murder by Medea may be assumed to have coexisted with the others from the time of Creophylus, so that in attributing the murder to Medea Euripides was simply choosing one available mythic tradition; thus, in Séchan's words, "Euripide n'aurait fait que l'accueillir et apporter une adhésion éclatante à l'une des thèses en présence dans un débat ouvert depuis longtemps."⁶ This school too has won significant adherents, gaining a status for itself, one might fairly say, as a notable minority opinion of twentieth-century scholarship. Among recent critics, Walter Burkert asserts that Medea was the original and deliberate killer: "That Medea, though inadvertently, killed her own children in the temple of Hera Akraia was already in Eumelos (Paus. 2.3.11); as it seemed strange that the Corinthians should atone for Medea's crime, the myth was altered to make the Corinthians the murderers of the children";[7] he is followed in this view by Pucci, who views the play as "the staging of the 'original' killing which is the *aition* of the Corinthian rituals."[8] Foley's unqualified acceptance of this aetiology suggests that, with another swing of the critical pendulum, Burkert's view may be starting to replace that exemplified by Page as the new orthodoxy, at least among a group of scholars concerned with the relationship of tragedy and sacrifice.[9] On the other hand, Page's view continues to garner support, as from Newton.[10]

The newer direction in Euripidean scholarship spurred by Burkert deserves careful attention; the evidence must be examined and evaluated in light of the counterclaims thus made against the older majority view represented by Page. To dispel suspense, let me say in advance that the posture which will underlie the present study is that, while the tangle of evidence is regrettably not susceptible to decisive resolution, examination of the sources will, on balance, draw the critic most reasonably to a working hypothesis that the deliberate child-murder by Medea was Euripides' innovation into the saga.

The evidence presented thus far in this chapter as productive of Page's inference concerning the mythic novelty of the deliberate child-murder leads to a line of argumentation which relies on the absence of contrary mythic evidence. That is, the absence of mythic material attesting to a pre-fifth-century tradition of Medea's deliberate slaying of her sons is taken as more than coincidental—as a lack so significant as to make an inference that such a tradition never existed more likely than the alternate conclusion that it did, but that any attestation to it has been lost. Evidence has on occasion been adduced from vase-painting and other areas of art in an attempt either to bolster or to refute such an argument; but this evidence is in itself subject to construction in opposite ways and so fails to add clarity.[11] Similarly, the connection of the various versions of the Medea-myth with the cult of Hera Acraea in Corinth, centered on the tomb of Medea's children, is too vexed by the chicken-and-egg ambiguities endemic to the relationship of myth and ritual to lead to any sure inference concerning the primacy of one or the other version of the tale.[12] Yet another set of variables is introduced by the interrelated questions of the nature of Medea's mythic connection to Corinth and of her own divine or mortal origins.[13]

Clearly, the case to be made on the basis of the type of argumentation described thus far—that is, an argument based on a lack of evidence otherwise—is neither definitive nor satisfying to those who must undertake it. However, a modicum of additional weight may be added to this generally inconclusive form of argument by a reflection that, in light of the relentless grip exerted after Euripides' time in both literature and art by the version of the tale in which the children's death is at their mother's premeditated agency, it seems rather unlikely that pre-Euripidean traces of this most appalling and psychologically compelling tradition would have just disappeared, leaving only the more prosaic, colorless versions of Eumelus, Creophylus, and Parmeniscus attested—if, that is, Euripides' tradition was indeed the original one.

Furthermore, one well-known piece of information (which Page presents but does not argue as specifically pertinent to the debate on innovation) provides us with a *terminus ante quem* for the onset of cultural amnesia of the pre-Euripidean appearance of a deliberately child-murdering Medea posited by Burkert. This is the story, attributed to Parmeniscus, that there existed a πολυάικος λόγος τῶν φιλοσόφων: "a widespread tale current among philosophers" that it was as a result of a bribe of five talents from the Corinthians (who in 431 b.c. were in open hostility to the Athenians) that Euripides transferred to Medea the murder which had traditionally been ascribed to their forefathers.[14] Scholars of all schools concerning innovation agree that no credence may be rested in the substance of this story (which Page dubs an "improbable fantasy" and Séchan an "absurde propos"). If it is true that it existed, however—and should one doubt Parmeniscus's testimony to that?—then it surely weakens Burkert's case: for such a rumor is obviously predicated on widespread ignorance of the purportedly original version of the myth. It thus indicates that the present lack of any pre-Euripidean sources attesting to the mother's deliberate child-murder cannot simply be attributed to the extensive gaps in preserved tradition which naturally plague modern scholars' attempts to investigate a culture which predates theirs by more than two thousand years. Rather, these "losses" in tradition had already occurred in antiquity, impelling scholars (*philosophoi*) who were removed from Euripides' time by closer to two hundred years to be swayed by a story which was an evident attempt to explain away the appearance in Euripides of an unfamiliar version of the Medea myth. Such an instance of mythic amnesia would be all the more startling in light of both the vastly greater mass of ancient source material available to the Alexandrian scholars than to us and the immense energy invested by them in researching and recording alternate and often arcane variations of myths.

To believe, with Burkert, that guilt in the children's death was early transferred to the Corinthians in an effort at rationalizing away the perceived anomaly of the ritual atonement by the Corinthians for Medea's crime thus entails as well presumption that, once that alteration occurred, all memory of the original anomalous version disappeared from received myth (whose intrinsic nature is distinctly to add, rather than to subtract, variants); then one is asked to believe that, despite the gripping and sensational substance of that original *aition*, its disappearance was effected to such a perfect degree that when it cropped up again its author could be slanderously said to have been bribed to foist off this untoward novelty on the fifth-century Athenian populace! The relative unlikelihood of such a process serves, in converse, to enhance the likelihood of the case which rests on the absence of extant attestation to a pre-Euripidean tradition of Medea's deliberate child-murder.

Finally, let me turn to examination of the nature and context of Burkert's conclusion that the crime imputed to Medea in Euripides' play is the original form of the story and the *aition* of the cult at the temple of Hera Acraea. Burkert is one of a group of recent scholars who have undertaken to study the perennially problematic question of the origins of tragedy in light of the fundamentally related subquestion of the relationship between tragic drama and sacrifice.[15] In the specific article in which the view quoted above appears, Burkert supports the hypothesis that the ancient etymology which connected *tragōidia* with a "song at the sacrifice of a goat" is an accurate reflection of the origins of the genre. He cites Medea's characterization of her impending crime as a "sacrifice" (*thumasin*: 1054) as one of three loci supportive of the integral connection between tragedy and sacrifice even at the time of the genre's maturity, and a locus particularly suited to defense of his major thesis, since the cult at the festival of Hera Acraea culminated in the sacrifice of a black she-goat.[16]

Burkert and others who have studied Greek sacrifice from a structuralist or evolutionist standpoint have succeeded in demonstrating that there exists an integral link between sacrifice and the genre of tragedy, a link which survives and is recurrently reflected in the genre's mature period. The exact nature of the original link is a matter which will continue both to absorb the attention of and to arouse unending dispute among scholars whose interests draw them from the literary back to the related sociological realities from which the literature has arisen. Within this context, the literary critic will continue to be drawn primarily to examination of the "facts" of the tragic text, however they came to be there—not that such examination can or should take place in a textual vacuum, sealed off from the historical and sociological context of Attic drama; but the literary critic's chief interest in the discourse undertaken by scholars of the sociological origins of the tragic genre will be what light may be shed on the artistic design of a tragic poet by careful analysis of the relationship between the genre's sociohistorical context and the sophisticated art of a poet of a mature literary genre. Unfortunately, study of this precise relationship is intrinsically hazardous, for one must promptly confront a whole complex of thorny issues revolving around authorial intent. For instance (to name only a few questions which arise): To what extent may the evidences of a primal link between sacrificial ritual and the plot-lines of fifth-century plays be taken as essentially passive vestiges of an earlier cultural reality? To what extent, on the other hand, may the author be assumed to be consciously asserting such a link for purposes of his own? To follow this line of questioning in a little more detail: if, as Burkert tells us, the motif of sacrifice was so pervasive in tragedy that *any* bloodletting could metaphorically come to be spoken of as a sacrifice, how are we to work our way out of the dilemma thus created, to decide whether any given reference to a sacrifice in drama arises from (and may be adduced as evidence for) the primal link between the two or is simply an instance where the playwright has drawn on a common pool of metaphor—whether in a neutral, unpointed way, and just as a manner of speaking, or to make a specific point about his characters' actions or states of mind? And finally, on a broader level, can the continuation of the motif of sacrifice be confidently taken (via a structural form of analysis) as indicator that the plays serve the same basic purpose (however the given critic chooses to define this elusive quality) as the ritual upon which they are based?[17]

The complexities of applying to explication of literary texts the insights to be gained from structuralist/evolutionist studies of the sacrificial origins of drama have been illuminatingly presented by Foley, who concisely pinpoints the literary critic's task as follows:

> The literary critic must in fact recognize, first, that tragic sacrifices, although they drew originally and continued in part to draw on an external model, may operate in ways that are not precisely comparable to the real event to which

they refer; and second, that the sacrificial metaphor had a complex independent development in tragic texts from Aeschylus to Euripides.[18]

At a later point in this study, a more detailed analysis of Euripides' use of the motif of sacrifice at lines 1054–55 will be to the point; for now, however, let us return specifically to Burkert's case for the primary nature of Medea's deliberate child-murder. It bears repeating that this hypothesis is a relatively small cog in Burkert's wheel: it is a single piece of evidence adduced to support his central thesis that tragedy is an offshoot of a ritual which revolves around the sacrificial death of a goat; as such, it is understandably not presented in a great deal of depth. Nevertheless, the supporting evidence cited by Burkert is extremely sparse. It consists of the unadorned appeal to post-Euripidean vase-paintings discussed in note 11 and of the similarly unadorned statement (quoted above) that the placing of guilt upon the Corinthians (as in Creophylus) was a later alteration to the myth motivated by an impulse to rationalize the Corinthians' ritual atonement for Medea's crime. The latter argument, though it is not devoid of verisimilitude, clearly requires substantiation beyond the citation of an imperfect mythic parallel in which Medea *inadvertently* causes her children's death. Why, for example, would such a rationalizing alteration not have been felt just as necessary to explain the Corinthians' atonement for an original *phonos akousios* by Medea?

Burkert further preserves a disturbing silence on the precise relationship he envisions between the issuance of a sacrificial metaphor from the lips of Euripides' character and the sacrificial origins of his genre. Given his failure to elaborate, one seems to be asked to read Medea's reference to sacrifice simply as a passive vestige of linkage between the Medea-saga and the cult at Hera Acraea; but, as that assumption may not do justice to the complexities of Euripides' penchant for deforming standard modes of thought and language, so the inclarity of the exact relationship posited by Burkert in this instance between the sociohistorical phenomenon of sacrifice and its metaphorical appearance in a literary text makes one doubly wary of accepting his conclusion.

In sum, the scantiness of both supporting evidence and argumentation presented by Burkert leads to a judgment that his case—though certainly not dismissible out of hand—is not substantial enough to counter the combined weight of the arguments presented above, predicated on the absence of pre-Euripidean mythic attestation of the purportedly original form of the myth.

Pucci accepts Burkert's conclusion that Medea was her children's murderer in the original form of the myth without himself entering into the discourse concerning the soundness of this postulate.[19] He does add important qualification to Burkert's thesis by elaborating on the workings of the sacrificial metaphor as an essentially literary device by the author.[20] Nonetheless, the critic who undertakes to test Page's inference that the child-murder was mythic innovation against Burkert's that it was the original tradition will find in Pucci no further argumentation to counter.[21]

At this point, let me present, in further support of the hypothesis that the deliberateness of the mother's killing of her children was an element introduced to the saga only in the fifth century, my own identification of two relevant passages from the text of the *Medea*.[22] Preliminarily, some background to the critical tradition within which the forthcoming analysis falls must be laid.

A 1969 article by Winnington-Ingram (see Introduction, note 13) may be viewed as the inaugural study of a series of articles which examine a particularly sophisticated type of Euripidean wit at the expense of the dramatic conventions which bind the tragedian. The prototypical example offered by Winnington-Ingram is that point in Euripides' *Electra* (759) where an anxious Electra, awaiting news of Orestes' attack on Aegisthus, finally concludes that Orestes must have failed, "For where are the messengers?" Winnington-Ingram notes the self-conscious glance contained in the character's query at the dramatic convention by which offstage violence is promptly reported to onstage characters through the arrival and report of a messenger.[23] Such anomalous breaches of dramatic convention are a keynote of comedy from Aristophanes down to modern times but are less naturally at home in the weightier genre of tragedy. Nonetheless, Winnington-Ingram has identified in Euripides a fondness for insertion of subtle bits of this sort of humor into his tragedies, imagining them as directed to the young, smart, and sophistically oriented set in his audience. Subsequent studies have appeared in similar mold.[24]

Just such a Euripidean witticism may be found at line 37 of the *Medea,* where the Nurse speaks words which contain the first of several foreshadowings that Medea will do harm to her children:[25]

στυγεῖ δὲ παῖδας οὐδ' ὁρῶσ' εὐφραίνεται.
δέδοικα δ' αὐτὴν μή τι βουλεύσῃ νέον.

> She hates the children and takes no joy in seeing them. I
> fear she may plan something untoward.
>
> (36–37)

The Greek phrase translated here as "something untoward" is *ti . . .
neon*. The word *neos*, which literally means "new," by a semantic
progression born of the conservative character of Greek culture became susceptible to the more sinister meanings "strange," "untoward," and "evil." It is this latter, pejorative set of meanings which
primarily attaches to the Nurse's phrase in line 37, as the Nurse hints
at some untoward action to come from a wronged and vengeful Medea. It is my contention, however, that under the surface meaning of
the character's words lurks a double entendre—"I am afraid she will
plan something *new*"—which points with disguised wit to the innovation into received myth to be introduced into the play when Medea
premeditatedly kills children who up till then had died either by
accident or at the hands of others. The aorist *bouleusēi* adds a further
refinement: "I am afraid she may light upon some strange new plan."
The Nurse's fear was to be proven well founded by the outcome of the
play.

It is, of course, common for characters in classical tragedy, in a form
of tragic irony, to utter words which are open to two levels of interpretation (see, e.g., Medea's address to her children at 1021ff.); but the
Nurse's ambiguity here proceeds one step further into artful contriv-
ance than normal, for her words' second meaning is achieved by a
breach of dramatic convention: the omniscient playwright speaks
here through an unknowing character (like Apollo through the
Pythia), and distinctly outside the bounds of tragic plot.

Euripides' suspenseful buildup, over almost eight hundred lines, to
Medea's eventual revelation to the Chorus and so to the audience that
her revenge on her enemies will entail the murder of her own children
(lines 792–93) will be discussed in some detail in the next chapter. I
will submit here the possibility that the playwright has introduced a
second double entendre, parallel to that contained in the Nurse's
phrase *ti . . . neon*, into the lines immediately preliminary to this momentous pronouncement.

Medea's account of her planned revenge turns first to description of
the strategy by which she will effect the death of the Corinthian
princess, using her children as unwitting agents (lines 774–89). She
then turns from this first aspect of her revenge, for which the Chorus

has been fully prepared by her earlier confidences to them, to the second and intensely shocking aspect of her plan:

ἐνταῦθα μέντοι τόνδ' ἀπαλλάσσω λόγον·
ᾤμωξα δ' οἷον ἔργον ἔστ' ἐργαστέον
τοὐντεῦθεν ἡμῖν· τέκνα γὰρ κατακτενῶ
τἄμ' . . .

There, however, I dismiss this story. But I grieve at the deed I must do thereafter—for I shall kill my children.

(790–93)

In a standard interpretation of line 790, Page glosses *tond' . . . logon* ("this story") as equivalent to "the content of 776–89."[26] Warner's translation sees in *logon* an accounting metaphor: "But there, however, I must leave that account paid."[27] In either view, the line serves essentially as a transitional formula, leading from one aspect of Medea's narrative to the next, but affording no significant substantive contribution to it. A neutral line, fallow field for the planting of double entendre. It is my suggestion that—just as he injected into the Nurse's first foreshadowing of the untoward path the myth would take at the end of his play an ever-so-subtle comment on that new direction—so here, at the precise point where the innovation is about to be openly proclaimed to Chorus and audience for the first time, he again disguises an allusion to his imminent departure from a more standard version of the story. "There, however, I quit this version of the story":[28] that is, "from this point forward (*tounteuthen*) I depart from a mythic track which would logically lead from my assault on the Corinthian king's house straight to the wreaking of vengeance by the angry Corinthians on my children. Instead, in my version, I will kill them myself." At the level of plot, Medea's announcement substantiates the Nurse's fearful prediction at line 37 ("I fear she may come upon some untoward plan"); at the extra-dramatic level, both the Nurse's and Medea's disguised double meanings constitute sophisticated authorial predictions of the turn to be taken by the plot and self-conscious comments on its novelty.

That these double entendres were intended by Euripides is not a matter which can be put to proof. However, it is at least remarkable that two lines so significantly located at points where the eventual outcome of the plot is in question are susceptible to parallel dual interpretation. When one adds that Euripides is increasingly seen by critics to have indulged a proclivity for bursting the conventional confines of his genre, the combination of these two observations may be taken as circumstantial evidence supportive of an inference that the deliberate child-murder was not an intrinsic element of the Medea-saga before Euripides' time and that Euripides, in adopting it, indirectly touts his own innovation.

In summary, while the evidence is neither abundant enough nor unambiguous enough that one may claim to have reached a definite answer to the question of whether Medea's purposeful attack on her children was an element introduced to her saga only in the fifth century, study of this evidence and of scholarly discourse concerning it has led this critic to adopt as working hypothesis the view that it was.

On the other hand, even if the original relationship of myth and ritual and the serial development of the myth were as Burkert posits (that the voluntary murder of the original myth was transferred to the Corinthians to explain the expiatory character of the cult at Corinth), one final point may be relevant. Euripides' plays—especially the quasi epilogues in which the mythic sequelae of the play's events are foretold and often, in turn, related by the playwright to contemporary cultic practices—make it clear that he was an avid student, even a "scholar," of myth, especially as it related to cult.[29] One may with some justification, then, speculate (again on the secondary assumption that Burkert's position on the suppression of an originally voluntary child-murder is correct) that Euripides may have come across an antiquated variant of the Medea-saga which was unfamiliar to the generality of his audience not only as a result of its lack of currency in their day but also because it was indigenous to Corinth rather than Athens. When, in that case, he chose to display that variant to them in his play, it would have had the same effect as if it had been a spontaneous innovation.

III

Unfortunately, the discussion concerning innovation may not even now be considered complete. Rather, we must first address in more detail the question of the provenance of the innovation. The second inference by Page referred to on page 00 above—that the presumed innovation concerning the child-murder is attributable directly to Euripides, rather than to Neophron—is widely accepted by modern scholars, who thereby decline to accept the charge of "plagiarism" leveled at Euripides in the Hypothesis of the play:

τὸ δρᾶμα δοκεῖ [ὁ Εὐριπίδης] ὑποβαλέσθαι παρὰ Νεόφρονος διασκευάσας, ὡς Δικαίαρχος... τοῦ τῆς Ἑλλάδος βίου καὶ Ἀριστοτέλης ἐν ὑπομνήμασι.

[Euripides] seems to have appropriated the plot from Neophron and revised it, as Dicaearchus says in the *Life of Greece* and Aristotle in the commentaries.

Nonetheless, assertion of Neophron's priority may never be considered dead, but only dormant.[30]

The "Neophron question" clearly adds insult to injury for one who would assess the question of mythic innovation in Euripides' plot: having come to a working hypothesis concerning the scantily attested pre-fifth-century traditions, the critic must face a second question which is fundamentally resistant to definitive resolution. While Thompson, in himself arguing for Neophron's priority, is obviously correct in asserting that most critics would *prefer* Euripides' version to precede Neophron's, they cannot justifiably be faulted for partiality when, *in the absence of a demonstrable case otherwise,* they indulge in that preferred hypothesis—any more than a critic who disputes the majority view of his time should be accused of doing so out of compulsive iconoclasm. As the evidence stands, the issue is simply not subject to decisive disposition. In fact, when one examines the meager evidentiary underpinnings for what has over the centuries been drawn out into an extended and extensive critical debate, what is most startling is not that a persuasive solution has not been found but that so many critics have felt ready to adopt dogmatic positions either way.

The evidence consists basically of (a) the Hypothesis's charge of plagiarism (quoted above), which in turn recurs in (b) Diogenes Laertius and (c) the Suda;[31] critics seem generally agreed that all mentions of the plagiarism most likely stem from a common source, the author of the Aristotelian *Hypomnemata* (as cited in the Hypothesis). The Suda (which is not notable for reliability) adds (d) that Neophron wrote 120 plays and was put to death by Alexander the Great (the executed man is elsewhere in the Suda called Nearchus). Finally, (e) three fragments of Neophron's *Medea* are preserved:[32] from the first we learn that Neophron provided closer motivation for Aegeus's arrival in Corinth than Euripides; the second is an address to Medea's *thumos* with strong affinities to the parallel Euripidean passage; from it we infer that Neophron too had Medea kill her children intentionally; in the third, Medea predicts that Jason will die by hanging, in contrast with the fate predicted for him by Euripides' character.

The testimony which intrinsically affects consideration of Neophron's date is the Suda's mutually contradictory assertions that he was the first to introduce certain elements to tragedy (see note 31) and that he was contemporary with Alexander. Critical suggestions of dates have, accordingly, most frequently been aimed at one or the other of the general times thus assigned to him, setting his *floruit* either around 470–460 or in the second half of the fourth century (Wilamowitz, on the other hand, disputes that he existed).

Thompson's plea for Neophron's anteriority is more notable for the damage it does to the case presented by those he would refute than for presentation of cogent and convincing evidence in his own behalf. Examination of his case, which in turn is constructed in the form of a refutation of Page, will provide a handy summary of the arguments generally made in this debate. Thompson's thesis rests on six evidentiary points.[33] Of these, three may be dismissed as misguided: (1) Thompson's assertion that "it is unlikely that a fourth-century Neophron would produce a very inferior adaptation of one of the greatest and most famous plays in existence at the time" is an argument notable more for hopeful assessment of the prudence to be imputed to those with literary aspirations than for persuasiveness in the world of fact. (2) Thompson's point that the coincidental nature of Aegeus's appearance onstage in Euripides' play is made explicable (and pardonable) by a presumption of the anteriority of his more closely motivated arrival in Neophron is not convincing. In line with Page, who in turn follows Séchan, I am inclined to lay more credence in the formulation that a derivative version more naturally seeks to pin down points of logic passed over in silence by an earlier treatment than the converse;[34] however, neither case may be made strongly enough to count as significant evidence.[35] (3) Even less cogent is the proposition that by assuming that Euripides was adapting an earlier play by Neophron we may explain the fact that Euripides' *Medea* requires only two actors at a date when Aeschylus and Sophocles had already introduced a third. Surely, no matter what the scale of Euripides' "appropriation" or "plagiarism" from Neophron, he would not have been such a limited or unimaginative technician that the staging technique of his model would necessarily have dictated his own; to argue for conscious archaism, intended to point with pride to his model, is too speculative to be convincing. No causal connection may be drawn with any confidence whatsoever between this oddity of the *Medea*'s production and the slippery question of Neophron's anteriority or posteriority. These three lines of argument by Thompson, it may be added, are not original to him but are already refuted by Séchan; Thompson's reassertion of them does not render them persuasive.

In a fourth area of argumentation, Thompson refutes in detail Page's adduction of peculiarities of diction in the fragments of Neophron as evidence for Neophron's posteriority. This form of argumentation by Page is one which has always aroused suspicions in this critic—suspicions which are regularly justified by the appearance of counterattacks discounting every judgment made in the original analysis. At any rate, Thompson's counterpoints are at least sufficient to call Page's conclusions into question; it should be emphasized, however, that they do not further Thompson's own case for Neophron's anteriority. Thus, while this section of Thompson's article has the negative effect of detracting from Page's case, it does not provide positive support for his own.

The two points made by Thompson which really have weight—and they are in fact equivalent to one—are that "the writer of the Aristotelian *Hypomnemata* says so" and that "it is otherwise difficult to see how his error could have originated."[36] Thompson's reasoning on this issue is, on balance, more compelling than Page's: it is difficult to imagine the fourth-century writer of the *Hypomnemata* getting so mixed up (whatever his talents as a literary critic) that he thought a Neophron who was writing in his own half century predated Euripides; but, again, demonstration of a weakness in Page's case is not tantamount to proof of one's own. The net effect of Thompson's article is to compound the reader's sense of the perplexity of the question.

No critic, to my knowledge, has suggested that Neophron might have been a rough contemporary of Euripides; in a field of inquiry where (in default of hard evidence) speculation in accordance with verisimilitude has been the order of the day, it may be noted that, if he were, two sources of difficulty would be alleviated: the confusion of a fourth-century commentator over which playwright wrote first would be understandable, and the points of diction in the fragments which Page identifies as clearly later than Aeschylus would be explained. The basic problem of which *Medea* preceded would remain; but perhaps one further speculation may be indulged here. For, even if Neophron's play did, in fact, precede Euripides', it does not follow necessarily that Euripides' audience would have prior knowledge of Neophron's plot, since a Sicyonian's work might have been known to a practitioner in the field but not to the general audience. In such a case, the effects of Euripides' play on his audience would have been the same as if Neophron had written nothing.

For the purposes of this study, Euripides' anteriority will be assumed as a working hypothesis on the grounds that arguments to the contrary are unconvincing and too weak to contravert a general sense that it is more likely that the lesser play is an imitation of the greater than vice versa; and that it seems prudent to relegate Neophron to status as an intriguing figure whose relation to Euripides is probably insoluble but can also be deemed with some justice irrelevant to evaluation of Euripides' work.

2

The Revelation

I

In analyzing the dramatic effect of Euripides' *Medea*, this study will treat the child-murder—not the bare fact of it, but the pervasive influence which audience realization of it and reaction to it have on the play's tone and meaning—as the central and indeed defining element of the play. Such an approach diverges radically from the view presented in the introduction to Page's important commentary on the play:

> Here, indeed, for the first time in the Greek theatre, the power of the drama lies rather in the characters than in their actions. Medea's emotions are far more moving than her revenge: Jason's state of mind is more interesting than his calamity. The murder of the children, caused by jealousy and anger against their father, is mere brutality: if it moves us at all, it does so towards incredulity and horror. Such an act is outside our experience; we—and the fifth-century Athenian—know nothing of it. But the emotions of the woman whose love has turned to hatred, and equally those of the man who loves no longer, represent something eternal and unchangeable in human nature;

> here we find, what in great drama we must always seek,
> the universal in the particular.[1]

While Page is correct that the child-murder impels primarily to incredulity and horror, his resultant desire to shunt it away from the center of the play could not be more misguided.[2] Rather, as will become clear, the play's dramatic technique is concentrated on the specific purposes of accentuating the impact of this unspeakable crime and of deliberately implanting and intensifying in the audience the precise sensations of incredulity and horror. Granting Page's point that we must seek the universal from literature, every clue drawn from Euripides' dramatic technique in this play indicates that the important universal point to be sought here is located not simply in the more familiar emotions of the parties to a bitter broken relationship, as Page suggests, but in the grotesque extremity of that bitterness's outcome in this particular case.

What is it that makes Medea's intention to kill her children so intrinsically horrifying? The maternal instinct to protect her young has been, across time, one of the most unchallenged and revered concepts of mankind. In fact, it is not unfair generalization to assert that most parents do feel an unutterably fierce and tender protectiveness toward their children; most nonparents can project a like emotion. Certainly the Athenians would not have challenged such a generalization. In fact, Aristotle makes more than one such categorical statement in his *Nicomachean Ethics* as he discusses the nature of the *philia* between parent and child: οἱ γονεῖς μὲν γὰρ στέργουσι τὰ τέκνα ὡς ἑαυτῶν τι (*Eth. Nic.* 8.12.2[1161ᵇ]): "For parents love their children as part of themselves . . .";[3] or again: γονεῖς μὲν οὖν τέκνα φιλοῦσιν ὡς ἑαυτούς (*Eth. Nic.* 8.12.3[1161ᵃ]): "Parents then love their children as themselves. . . ." The larger context within which these generalizations fall is Aristotle's discussion of the reciprocally enjoined nurture, or *trophē*, which characterized the workings of the Greek family as a societal unit. In brief, the *trophē* which the parent expends on the child in the latter's time of helplessness is seen as a kind of debt to be repaid by the child when the parent is returned to helplessness by age. Discussion of the thematic importance of this value to the *Medea* will be central to chapters 5 and 6 of this study; here it is of importance primarily in that Aristotle's discussion of the concept sheds some light on one particular aspect of what may be presumed to be a general Greek attitude about parental love. That is, whereas the return made to the parent by the child is seen not as a human "given," but as a duty required of him by a strict societal code, the impulse of the parent to care for the child is viewed as so natural as to be unexceptionable—except in rare cases where the child has merited renunciation through his own personal *mochthēria:* "depravity."[4] A parallel fundamental presumption is clearly at work in Hesiod's *Works and Days*. There Hesiod cites failure of reciprocal child-to-parent return of *trophē* as a phenomenon of his most deteriorated generation:

αἶψα δὲ γηράσκοντας ἀτιμήσουσι τοκῆας·
μέμψονται δ' ἄρα τοὺς χαλεποῖς βάζοντες ἔπεσσι,
σχέτλιοι, οὐδὲ θεῶν ὄπιν εἰδότες· οὐδέ κεν οἵ γε
γηράντεσσι τοκεῦσιν ἀπὸ θρεπτήρια δοῖεν.

And forthwith they will dishonor their aging parents; they will blame them, speaking with harsh words—hardhearted, and with no thought to the vengeance of the gods; nor would these give their aged parents return for their nurture.

(*Op.* 185–88)

Hesiod sees default by the child on the debt owed to the parent as one symptom of the disease of the iron race. His silence concerning even the possibility of the converse—failure of the parent to provide initial *trophē* to the child—is eloquent: such an eventuality was apparently beyond the pale of even the worst age foreseen by Hesiod.

That natural parental *philia* was further attributed by the Greeks most particularly to female parents is also apparent. It was a cliché in fifth-century Athens, just as it is now, that no matter how mild or savage the animal, the female of the species will be characterized by fierce protectiveness toward its young.[5] Within the human realm, the many literary expressions of the myth of Iphigenia's sacrifice by her father for the "masculine" motives of war lust and ambition and her mother's subsequent vengeance upon her husband may be named as a fecund source for a generalization by the Greeks concerning the strength of mother-love. Especially notable in a study of Euripides is his portrayal in the *Iphigenia Aulidensis* of a highly sympathetic, pre-sacrifice Clytemnestra, championing her child's cause against her husband. Further support is available from the Athenians' own theoretical discourse on this question. For instance, the Aristotelian passage excerpted above contains the observation that ἐκ τούτων δὲ δῆλον καὶ δι' ἃ φιλοῦσι μᾶλλον αἱ μητέρες: "These considerations also explain why parental affection is stronger in the mother" (*Eth. Nic.* 8.12.3 [1161ᵇ]). Xenophon expounds a similar thesis in his retailing of the ways in which god has differentiated male and female:

τῇ δὲ γυναικὶ ἧττον τὸ σῶμα δυνατὸν πρὸς ταῦτα φύσας τὰ ἔνδον ἔργα αὐτῇ, φάναι ἔφη, προστάξαι μοι δοκεῖ ὁ θεός. εἰδὼς δέ, ὅτι τῇ γυναικὶ καὶ ἐνέφυσε καὶ προσέταξε τὴν τῶν νεογνῶν τέκνων τροφήν, καὶ τοῦ στέργειν τὰ νεογνὰ βρέφη πλεῖον αὐτῇ ἐδάσατο ἢ τῷ ἀνδρί.

To the woman, since he has made her body less capable of such [i.e., manly] endurance, I take it that God has assigned the indoor tasks. And knowing that he had created in the woman and had imposed on her the nourishment [*trophē*] of the infants, he meted out to her a larger portion of affection for newborn babes than to the man.[6]

(*Oec.* 7.23–24)

A line of discourse concerning parentage which begins (among extant sources) in Homer's *Odyssey* is indicative of a related assumption on the part of Greek culture that the tie between mother and child was not only an inherently close one, but was also the primary social tie. In the first book of the *Odyssey*, Telemachus responds to a question concerning his parentage with a somewhat surprising remark: τοιγὰρ ἐγώ τοι, ξεῖνε, μάλ᾽ ἀτρεκέως ἀγορεύσω. / μήτηρ μέν τ᾽ ἐμέ φησι τοῦ ἔμμεναι, αὐτὰρ ἐγώ γε / οὐκ οἶδ᾽· οὐ γάρ πώ τις ἐὸν γόνον αὐτὸς ἀνέγνω: "I will tell you truly, stranger: in fact, my mother says I am his [Odysseus's] son, but I for my part do not know, for no one yet has known his father on his own" (*Od.* 1.214–16). Telemachus does not, of course, mean to call his mother's touted fidelity into question; his words are, rather, philosophical, evoking an early stage of Greek thought on socialization which took the mother-child tie, the most fundamental—in fact, the only truly knowable—blood connection between human beings, as the first building block for the more elaborate social constructs of a later stage of civilization. Anthropologists will tell us that in the very primitive stages of a society the connection may not be made between intercourse and pregnancy; thus "paternity" is not in such a beginning even a known concept. Telemachus's words obviously well postdate any such primitive period, but they are nonetheless predicated on the tenet that maternity is the first of social ties. At a more "advanced" stage in Greek civilization, Aeschylus will have

the Apollo of his *Eumenides* make a case, by contrast, that the fa
the primary parent: using rationalistic arguments in his confro
with the maternalistic, blood-tie-oriented Furies, the "young" Olympian will seek to counter the more fundamental and prevailing opinion that the mother-child tie is the most basic familial bond, in order
to ratify a paternalistic set of values. Neither the specifics nor the
merits of his case are at issue here; it is relevant only in that, as an
elaborately and artificially rationalized attempt to supplant a more
orthodox mode of thought, it adumbrates the primacy attached by the
generality of Greek thought to the bond between mother and child.

It is further notable that in Euripides' Athens the *aretē* of a woman
was defined strictly and narrowly by her successful fulfillment of the
role of bearer of children and protectress of the household. Such is the
lesson to be preached, for example, by the excursus of Xenophon
cited above, in which fifth-century Athenian social mores are ratified
by appeal to an intrinsic differentiation between the god-given character of male and female. In the context of this perceived confluence
between the inborn maternal nature of the female character and her
societally appointed "profession," then, the repulsion engendered by
the child-murdering mother would be especially acute.

At lines 811ff. of the *Medea*, when the Chorus (which has up to that
time been willingly complicit in Medea's plans for revenge) learns that
those plans entail the murder of her own children, they invoke the
nomoi brotōn: "laws of humankind" to dissuade Medea from her unnatural proposition:

σέ τ' ὠφελεῖν θέλουσα, καὶ νόμοις βροτῶν
ξυλλαμβάνουσα, δρᾶν σ' ἀπεννέπω τάδε.

From a desire to help you as well as to foster the laws of
humankind, I bid you, do not do this.

(812–13)

Given the value placed by the Athenians on the family as the base of
social order, the portrayal of a wife who will break the most sacred
human tie—the very cornerstone of the *nomoi brotōn*—simply to devastate her husband must be an especially terrifying figure. And it must
also be conceded that the sins of the husband which prompted this
revenge were not so great in the eyes of the author's society. Jason's
"crimes" were merely divorce and breach of the oaths by which Medea had bound him at the time of their marriage (see lines 161–62).

Divorce was a completely commonplace affair in fifth-century Athenian society, involving merely the dissolution of the "fact" of marriage; breach of oaths, though a crime, was one whose punishment would be expected to issue in some unspecific way and at some unspecific time from gods like Themis and Zeus (169–70; cp. 208), and was not just cause for murder or atrocity by the offended party.[7] No matter how much we may indict Jason for his ingratitude, his weaselly manner, and his self-interested rationalizations, he is no worse, really, than the middling man. A cad, yes; a criminal, no.

Additionally, Philip Slater's analysis of social structure and family dynamics in fifth-century Athens may be of use in further assessing the effects that the introduction into the Medea-saga of the mother's purposeful murder of her male children would have upon an Athenian audience. Slater draws a psychological portrait of a fifth-century Athenian mother who—isolated and restricted by the confines of her home, while her older, more educated husband ranged freely among the multifarious political, cultural, and personal possibilities afforded by his society—habitually vented her resentment of the social and sexual double standard on her male children in their formative years, when they were totally within their mother's sphere of domination. Alternately prizing her sons and despising them for their male sex (that is, visiting on the children her own ambivalent reactions of admiration and resentment for her absentee husband), this mother might well afflict her male offspring with a latent sense of the contradictorily nurturing and destructive potential of the Mother-figure.[8] Both Slater's adduction of this phenomenon as cause for the Athenian societal predilection for male homosexuality and his support of his theory by means of myths which were created a thousand years before and in a societal structure far different from fifth-century Athenian society arouse suspicion.[9] Nonetheless, the picture he paints of the mother-son relationship in Euripides' Athens may help to illuminate some aspects of the *Medea*'s artistry.

Responding to Page's comment that the murder of children is "outside our experience" and that of the fifth-century Athenian, Easterling cites the startling statistical frequency with which, in modern times, children are murder victims, predominantly of their parents, and queries: "May it not be that in *Medea* we find Euripides exhibiting the same psychological sureness of touch as in his studies of Phaedra and Electra and Pentheus, or as in the scene where Cadmus brings Agave back to reality?"[10] This suggestion is clearly to the point. Indeed, it is the very fact that Medea's murder of her children seems psychopathologically possible, even convincing, both to us and to an ancient audience, that renders it as horrible as it is. Add to Easterling's observations on timeless human behavior Slater's additional insights into the pathological profile to which the mother-son relationship was susceptible in fifth-century Athens in particular, and it becomes clearer that, faced with Medea's unspeakable actions, the Athenian audience would be hard put to feel that the power of this drama lay elsewhere but in those actions. It is Aristotle's famous formulation that tragedies are designed to arouse in their audiences not only pity (*eleos*) for the suffering of the hero but fear (*phobos*) born of the realization that all men are subject to a like fate (*Poetics* 6.1449[b].24ff.; cp. 13.1453[a].2ff.). If one applies this formulation to the outcome of the *Medea*, it is a fair inference that any even slight recognition by a male audience member of silently smoldering resentment in his own or others' housebound women might be precipitated by this catalyst into queasy *phobos* for himself, his sex, and the social order of fifth-century Athens.

Page explains away the extremity of Medea's revenge against Jason by accidents of her birth and maintains that the fear she engenders would thus be assuaged:

> The Athenian audience was neither incredulous of the murder nor critical of the magic chariot. Παμφάρμακος ξείνα ["foreign woman adept in every drug"] was Pindar's description of Medea. Because she was a foreigner she could kill her children; because she was a witch she could escape in a magic chariot. She embodies the qualities which the fifth-century Athenian believed to be characteristic of Orientals. Jason himself understood the truth in the end: οὐκ ἔστιν ἥτις τοῦτ' ἂν Ἑλληνὶς γυνὴ ἔτλη ποθ' ["there is no Greek woman who would ever have dared this"].[11]

While Page is clearly correct that Medea's non-Greek roots are suspect (see below, p. 47), his assertion that she may therefore murder her children without outraging the audience's universal humanity is remarkably ill-conceived. Throughout this play, Euripides goes out of his way precisely to inspire horror in his audience at the mother's unnatural act; he certainly does not mean for them to shuck that horror off by concluding that it applies to women of one geographical provenance only. While the recurrent mentions of Medea's alien status may provide token alleviation,[12] try as they might, the Athenian audience would not be able to escape completely the uneasy sense that Medea's crime is of wider applicability than they would like to think, and that her fury threatens their safe Greek world as well. As Reckford has said: ". . . Euripides seems unmistakably to surprise his audience with the awareness that pressures analogous to those working upon Medea exist in their own comfortable homes."[13] One sure indicator that the case is such is found, in fact, in the very line which Page cites to support his opposite conclusion. When, at the end of the play (1339–40), Jason hurls at Medea the charge that no Greek woman would ever have committed such an act, his assertion has a hollow ring. Ino, the single parallel cited by the Chorus at lines 1282ff., was assuredly a Greek woman; Procne, whom the audience would inevitably supply as an additional parallel from their own mental store of received myth, was not only Greek, but Athenian (see below, pages 46ff.). The irony, then, that Jason's insularly patriotic assertion here is patently incorrect would surely be sensible by Euripides' audience— even if they would have liked to believe this hopeful assessment of the situation. Finally, it should be noted, with Knox, that in Page's long catalogue of "tales as bad as this or worse" from Oriental history, there still is no truly parallel example: he has apparently found no report of a non-Greek mother murdering her own children.[14]

Assuming, then, that the fact of the child-murder will ultimately be absolutely central to the audience's experience of the play, we must next examine how the playwright leads them to that climax. Two essential questions must be asked: first, how the revelation that the children are to be cold-bloodedly murdered by their mother is made to the audience of Euripides' *Medea* and, second, what effect that revelation would have on them. From this point forward, my primary arguments will be based on the working hypothesis that Medea's deliberate murder of her children was indeed Euripides' own innovation into the saga;[15] where it seems appropriate, I shall introduce secondary arguments predicated on differing assumptions. Ultimately, however, the question of whether Euripides was forging completely new mythic ground here is inessential to the forthcoming presentation of the revelation process perpetrated by the author and undergone by the audience. While clearly the horror of Medea's murder of her innocent children will be the most intensely *shocking* to the audience if one adopts the hypothesis that it was new to them, the account of the revelation process to be presented here rests (even more than on shock) on the creation of tormenting suspense in the audience, through the alternation of clues to the play's outcome which lead in opposite directions. This facet of the unraveling of the plot pertains whether or not the audience was aware at the outset of deliberate murder as a mythic option available to the poet.

II

The prologue spoken by the Nurse at the beginning of the *Medea* quickly and concisely informs the audience that the scene of the play is Corinth, the site of Jason's exile from Iolcus; its subject: the final break-up of Medea and Jason's marriage. Medea's initial amorous enthrallment to Jason, the Fleece, and the atrocity perpetrated on Pelias are things of the past; her interlude with Aegeus lies in the future.[16]

The scene-setting prologue (1–48) establishes a grim and foreboding tone: a contrary-to-fact wish that Jason and Medea might never have met is followed swiftly by a grim one-line assessment of the present state of affairs:

νῦν δ' ἐχθρὰ πάντα, καὶ νοσεῖ τὰ φίλτατα.

But as it is, everything is hateful, and the family [*ta philtata*: see Glossary] is diseased.

(16)

Jason's betrayal of Medea and his children is sketched briefly (17–19). The text then continues with a lengthy description (20–45) of Medea's reactions—a tone poem on paralyzing grief and betrayal, which sounds the first warning note of the actual revenge to come. This first hint of the bizarre direction Euripides intends Medea's revenge to take comes in the Nurse's words at lines 36–37:

στυγεῖ δὲ παῖδας οὐδ' ὁρῶσ' εὐφραίνεται.
δέδοικα δ' αὐτὴν μή τι βουλεύσῃ νέον.

She hates the children and takes no joy in seeing them. I fear she may plan something untoward.

Those who in fact know the play's ending may tend to see these lines not as a hint only, but as a clear prediction of the coming turn of events. Considered in its broader context, however, this hint is nowhere near so bald as it appears when quoted as a two-line excerpt, as above. The Nurse's recital of Medea's plight turns directly from a quick summary of the facts of Jason's defection (16–19) to a more detailed account of Medea's reaction to that defection. From lines 20–29 she is viewed as crying out passionately against her husband's faithlessness; from lines 30–35 she looks back to her father and her homeland and laments the loss of protection from that quarter; at line 36 she is said to take no joy even from her children. From this sequence of thought, it is clear that Medea's overall reaction to Jason's departure partakes of a tripartite structure (comprising segments of unequal length), in which the destruction of her family unit is seen serially through its relation to one family tie after another: husband, father, sons. Such a progression of thought not only is emotionally convincing but is lent added point by the Athenian sociological patterns during Euripides' own time, by which a woman—deemed utterly helpless on her own—would look first to her husband for support; once denied there (as in a divorce situation), her first recourse would be to revert to her father for guardianship; if that way were barred too (as it was for Medea), she would naturally turn to her male children for protection.

This sequence of thought (husband-father-sons) is complete after line 36. With line 37, the Nurse proceeds on a new tack: "Since Medea has no comfort or recourse from these traditional sources, I fear she will do something untoward." From her next words (lines 38–45), in which she elaborates on Medea's terrible and vengeful character, it is fully apparent that what the Nurse has in mind here is potential action by Medea against those who have wronged her, rather than against her children.[17] The conjunction of the two ideas, "children" and "untoward response" (*ti . . . neon*), then, is not so close as to constitute a clear statement of prophecy. It certainly is sufficiently sinister to remind the audience that in *no* mythic variant do the children survive Medea's Corinthian episode; but any in the audience with time and wit to think ahead at this point in the plot would most likely be drawn to anticipate vengeance by Medea on one or more of the Jason-Creon-Creusa[18] trio, followed by Medea's escape and her children's death at the hands of the vengeful Corinthians (cp. the account in Creophylus). The children's accidental death through some fault of their mother might somehow be worked in, but it would have to be in a different form from that reconstructed from Pausanias's elliptical allusion, since that rests on the presumption that it was their death and Medea's guilt in it which turned Jason from Medea in the first place—a detail patently at odds with the Nurse's sketch of Jason's disaffection at lines 17ff. At any rate, regardless of which mythic variant they might most bring to mind, these words by the Nurse constitute the first of several tantalizing hints proffered to the audience— hints which, taken together, establish a pattern of foreshadowing.[19]

As soon as this first hint has been dropped, the children promptly arrive onstage; their innocence is emphasized (νέα γὰρ φροντὶς οὐκ ἀλγεῖν φιλεῖ: "For the young mind is not used to feeling pain" [48]). When the *Paidagōgos* is addressed ceremoniously by the Nurse as τέκνων ὀπαδὲ πρέσβυ τῶν Ἰάσονος: "aged attendant of Jason's sons" (53), the alert audience member will begin to feel something of the same edginess voiced in a different play by Polonius ("still harping on my daughter"): there is just too much emphasis on the children for it to be unmotivated.[20] The audience is thus signaled both that the compass of this play will include the children's death in Corinth, which is surely foreknown to them as a mythic "fact," and that these children will play some sort of important role in the unfolding of the action to come; but the *nature* of that role is still unclear. They still might most likely be reminded of the mythic prototypes in which the children are killed by the angry Corinthians or of those in which Medea accidentally brings about her children's death in some manner (or perhaps of some combination of the two). For—beyond the one unspecific hint at lines 36–37—there has been no indication that willful harm to the children by their mother is what impends. A clearer, and rapid-fire, series of foreshadowings begins at line 89. In two speeches (89–95 and 98–110), the Nurse hurries the children inside and away from their mother's sight and expresses her fear that Medea's savage anger may fall on the innocent, rather than on those who have wronged her (ἐχθρούς γε μέντοι, μὴ φίλους, δράσειέ τι: "But may she take action against her enemies, not her friends" [95]). In lines 112–13, Medea herself curses the children as born from a hated union; the Nurse responds with renewed anxiety for the children's safety (οἴμοι, / τέκνα, μή τι πάθηθ᾽ ὡς ὑπεραλγῶ: "Alas, children, how grieved I am that you may suffer wrong" [117–18]).

Contrapuntal to this intensifying sense of foreboding, however, is the more explicitly stated theme that it is Jason who is the betrayer of his children. He is flatly condemned as such by the Nurse as early as lines 17–18 (προδοὺς γὰρ αὑτοῦ τέκνα δεσπότιν τ᾽ ἐμὴν / γάμοις Ἰάσων βασιλικοῖς εὐνάζεται: "For Jason beds down in royal wedlock, betraying my mistress and his own sons"), and, in the later conversation of the Nurse and the *Paidagōgos*, Jason's heartless relegation of his sons

to exile is anticipated (see especially lines 74–75) and generalized into
an exemplification of the faithlessness and egocentricity of mankind:

Τρ. ὦ τέκν᾽, ἀκούεθ᾽ οἷος εἰς ὑμᾶς πατήρ;
ὄλοιτο μὲν μή· δεσπότης γάρ ἐστ᾽ ἐμός·
ἀτὰρ κακός γ᾽ ὢν ἐς φίλους ἁλίσκεται.
Πα. τίς δ᾽ οὐχὶ θνητῶν; ἄρτι γιγνώσκεις τόδε,
ὡς πᾶς τις αὑτὸν τοῦ πέλας μᾶλλον φιλεῖ, . . .
εἰ τούσδε γ᾽ εὐνῆς οὕνεκ᾽ οὐ στέργει πατήρ.

Nurse: O children, do you hear how your father treats
you? I will not curse him, for he is my master; but he is
caught out behaving basely toward his kin.
Paidagōgos: Is it ever otherwise? Have you only now come
to realize that everyone loves himself more than his neighbor, . . . if for the sake of his bed the father fails to cherish
these boys.

(82–88)

This theme of Jason's faithlessness tugs in the opposite direction to
the pattern of foreshadowing which hints that Medea will be her
children's destroyer. The opposition of these two themes must have
affected the audience with uncertainty as to which set of clues they
should believe. Their dilemma continues when, after the rapidly accel-
erating set of hints that Medea's vengeance or its results will fall in
some fashion on her children (lines 89–118), the next set of clues again
points in two different directions. While Medea's explicit musings on
her future course turn first to suicide (145–47), then to unelaborated
fantasies of death for Jason and his bride (ὅν ποτ᾽ ἐγὼ νύμφαν τ᾽
ἐσίδοιμ᾽ / αὐτοῖς μελάθροις διακναιομένους: "May I some day see him
and his bride destroyed, house and all" [163–64]), the Chorus (173ff.)
echoes the Nurse's earlier apprehensions by taking action to guard
against Medea's wrath falling upon *tous eisō:* "the ones within [Me-
dea's house]" (183).[21]

To sum up: from the beginning of the play through Medea's entry
onto the stage at line 214, the audience is proffered two conflicting
sets of clues concerning the eventual direction of Medea's revenge (it
is never in doubt that she *will* exact vengeance). On the one hand,
her wrath is foreseen as falling—appropriately—on some or all of the
triangle of offenders, Jason, the princess, and Creon; on the other, a
strong pattern of foreshadowing hints that Medea's wrath will in

some way—inappropriately, the audience must feel, and perhaps only inadvertently—cause the destruction of her own children. But further distracting from this pattern of foreshadowing is the concurrent, explicitly sounded theme that Jason is his children's betrayer, not Medea. Euripides is deliberately playing with his audience's expectations, teasing them, toying with them, in such a way as to heighten their feeling of suspense and their anxiety to know the resolution.

Once Medea enters the stage at line 214, however, the picture changes. First, this onstage Medea is different from the one reported secondhand by the Nurse and heard in brief snatches crying out her pain. This Medea is in control: cold, analytical, calculating. If we were alert, we might immediately sense that she has progressed from passive reaction to an active stage in her response to Jason's betrayal.[22] Second, the foreshadowings concerning the children are halted; Medea's "explicit" statement of her plans pulls our expectations away from the idea of harm to her children, and in another, more apparently logical direction: action against Jason *et al.*

In fact, from the time of her entrance until line 792, when she finally drops her bombshell on the Chorus (τέκνα γὰρ κατακτενῶ / τἄμ': "for I shall kill my children" [792–93]), there is no further hint that the mother will in some way turn upon her children. Rather, the poet seems to be taking great care to point the other direction, as if to erase from the audience's minds the sinister seeds he has so carefully sown. By thus temporarily allaying the suspicions he has roused in his audience through the play's first two hundred lines, the playwright sets them up for a ruder shock when Medea reveals her true plan.

In Medea's first speech to the Corinthian women, she speaks of her own humiliation and perilous plight, and—calling upon their empathy as women, who will understand the depth of the wrongs done by men—she begs their complicity in exacting vengeance upon Jason (ἢν μοι πόρος τις μηχανή τ' ἐξευρεθῇ / πόσιν δίκην τῶνδ' ἀντιτείσασθαι κακῶν, / [. . .] / σιγᾶν: "if I can find some way and means to punish my husband for these wrongs, . . . remain silent" [260–63]). The Chorus responds that such vengeance is entirely suitable and agrees to her terms. When Creon confronts Medea, he admits openly that he is afraid—first for his own child (μή μοί τι δράσῃς παῖδ' ἀνήκεστον κακόν: "lest you do my child some irrevocable harm" [283]), then for himself and Jason along with her (287–89). All this emphasis on the potentiality of revenge by Medea on Jason and his new family (the *proper* targets for her hatred) has the effect of distracting from the apprehension so carefully implanted in the audience's minds before the appearance of Medea onstage that Medea's anger will somehow vent itself (improperly) on her children. The assertion of a mother's tender protectiveness toward her children on which Medea bases her appeal to Creon for a day's grace, playing on his own clearly tender paternal feelings (οἴκτιρε δ' αὐτούς· καὶ σύ τοι παίδων πατὴρ / πέφυκας: "Pity them; you too are the father of children" [344–45]), will be revealed by her eventual course of action to have been fiendishly hypocritical; but at this point in the dramatic action the audience could not be sure of her feelings. They are purposely suspended by the playwright in a state of doubt. Should they believe the *character*? That is, should they assume that, despite any tendency to deceit they may already have noted in the heroine,[23] she must at least be genuine in her statement of overriding concern for her children (τοὐμοῦ γὰρ οὔ μοι φροντίς, εἰ φευξούμεθα, / κείνους δὲ κλαίω συμφορᾶ κεχρημένους: "For my thought is not for myself, and the question of my exile; rather I weep for these boys, sunk in misfortune" [346–47])? Her charge of Jason's heartless lack of concern for his sons (ἐπεὶ πατὴρ / οὐδὲν προτιμᾶ μηχανήσασθαι τέκνοις: "since their father does not choose to provide for his children" [342–43]) is certainly credible, as it reechoes the earlier analysis of his actions by the Nurse and the *Paidagōgos*. Or should they "believe" the earlier foreshadowings: in other words, should they trust that the playwright will actually carry through on the unspecific course of action he has hinted at through the repeated conjunction of the ideas of "children" and "revenge"? The way is still unclear; they are forced to suspend judgment.

Those who would resist the presentiment of a child-murdering mother are tendered one seemingly more tangible support in Medea's subsequent statement to the Chorus that, in the one day's reprieve Creon has foolishly granted her,

> . . . τρεῖς τῶν ἐμῶν ἐχθρῶν νεκροὺς
> θήσω, πατέρα τε καὶ κόρην πόσιν τ' ἐμόν.

> I shall make corpses of my three enemies—the father, the girl, and my husband.

(374–75)

She states explicitly here that the form her revenge will take is murder of the three offending parties themselves. In this statement, she reveals her previous wheedling of Creon as fawningly manipulative.

Paradoxically, that revelation has the effect of disarming the audience's anxiety for her children. After Creon's departure from the stage, one naturally expects a greater degree of candor from her; she seems to supply it, by dropping her pretenses and openly proclaiming her plans for revenge. Like the Chorus, the audience is lulled into a false confidence that Medea has now revealed—to *them*, if not to Creon (a standard dramatic technique)—the nature and extent of her true intentions.[24] They are being manipulated by the playwright (again, much as the Chorus is by Medea) into a too hasty conclusion that they may have been wrong in picking up on those earlier "clues" that Medea was going to do something terrible to her children. The sense of foreboding aroused by the foreshadowings concerning the children would not be erased by the bald statement that Medea's spite will be vented on Jason, Creon, and the princess; but the most likely supposition to be made at this point in the narrative is that the playwright will draw here on mythic variants which involve revenge on the children by the Corinthians (i.e., as an *inadvertent* result of their mother's actions).

As the play continues, the eventual fate of the children remains wrapped in silence; there are no renewed foreshadowings. That is not to say, however, that the child-theme itself is completely dropped.[25] The subject of their status figures centrally in Jason and Medea's vituperative dialogue (446–626), as each one accuses the other of selfish lack of parental concern. The episode between Medea and Aegeus likewise centers on the subject of children: that is, Aegeus's yearning for his own. But this thematic continuity is so subtle that, beyond a subliminally heightened awareness of the parent-child relationship as a theme, recognition of it comes only upon retrospection. Otherwise, there is no repetition of the previous dark hints about the children's fate until Medea finally proclaims her true plan (774ff.). Using her own innocent children as unwitting agents, she will kill the princess. So far, so good; we have "known" that some such murder will take place since Medea's announcement of her intended triple murder at lines 374–75; all the emphasis on the children to date has prepared us for their assumption of some role in the revenge; and, finally, their use as tools of Medea's revenge would lead appropriately to a conclusion in which, in line with received myth (or at the very least with one vein of it), they are in turn murdered by the angry Corinthians. But our expectations are rudely affronted when she goes on from here to plot subsequent death *not* for Creon and Jason, but—to the horror of both Chorus and audience—for her own sons:

ᾤμωξα δ᾽ οἷον ἔργον ἔστ᾽ ἐργαστέον
τοὐντεῦθεν ἡμῖν· τέκνα γὰρ κατακτενῶ
τἄμ᾽· οὔτις ἔστιν ὅστις ἐξαιρήσεται.

But I grieve at the deed I must do thereafter—for I shall kill
my children; there is no one who can save them.

(791–93)

The effect on the audience must have been electric; one can imagine
involuntary cries of protest: *No!* and *Why?*

Medea answers the latter directly. In place of simple murder, in
Jason's case she has substituted a more diabolically apropos punishment. By rejecting her, Jason has destroyed her home: καὶ πᾶς δόμος
ἔρροι: "May the whole house fall," Medea prays in the offstage laments preceding her initial entrance onto the stage (114); οὐκ εἰσὶ
δόμοι: "There is no house," echoes the Nurse (139). Now Medea will
do the same for his, δόμον τε πάντα συγχέασ᾽ Ἰάσονος . . .: "demolish-
ing Jason's entire house" (794). For the Greek male, the primary familial duty was to have sons to carry on his family line. Medea has
already cast in Jason's teeth the inexcusability of his seeking marriage
with another woman when he already had sons (παίδων γεγώτων
[490]). Now she will punish him by rendering him perpetually *apais*—
perhaps the worst fate which could be visited upon the Greek male:

οὔτ᾽ ἐξ ἐμοῦ γὰρ παῖδας ὄψεταί ποτε
ζῶντας τὸ λοιπὸν οὔτε τῆς νεοζύγου
νύμφης τεκνώσει παῖδ᾽, ἐπεὶ κακῶς κακὴν
θανεῖν σφ᾽ ἀνάγκη τοῖς ἐμοῖσι φαρμάκοις.

For he will neither see his sons by me alive in the future
nor beget a child by his newly wedded wife, since she
must altogether die, a horrible death, by my drugs.

(803–6)

All audiences feel the affront that a mother's murder of her own
flesh and blood is both repugnant and unnatural. That Medea's undertaking of this crime is motivated not by an uncontrollable surge of
violent feeling against the children themselves but by a coldly calcu-
lated reckoning of how to inflict maximum mental pain on Jason
makes us shudder at the pathological depths to which the human
mind can sink. If, however, it is the case that Euripides was the first to

introduce this element to the saga, it is additionally true that the sense of outrage felt by the original Athenian audience at Medea's revelation can be fully appreciated only as refracted through their normal expectations of a playwright with regard to received myth. If, by tradition, Medea is not expected to murder her children, then the revelation to the Athenian audience that that is what she *will* do is fraught with a double affront: not only that shared by modern audiences, but also a sudden realization that Euripides is here stretching the bonds of mythic tradition.

The most evident effect of the playwright's alteration of the received mythic tradition is the presentation of a degenerated heroine. Character degeneration, concomitant with the demythologization of heroes, was a device favored by Euripides as a means of communicating the seemingly infinite potential of human fallibility and, concurrently, of manipulating his audience's emotions through the violence he does to characterizations they have come to accept as true. Audience response to this technique, I have suggested elsewhere, was likely to partake of a range of negative emotions—from a sense of loss to moral repugnance to irascible resistance to the playwright's attempt to wrench them from their previously ingrained assessment of the rights and wrongs of a mythical figure's character and/or situation and so to convince them, willy-nilly, not only that the "good" may really be bad, but also that their "truths" are illusory rather than abiding.[26] Whatever the mythic precedents, when Euripides has Medea purposefully commit this most extreme crime, he in effect tells his audience not to trust in any prescriptions of human morality or any statement of natural order, for the *real* story is that "heroes" are just people, and people will stoop to anything. If, additionally, it was the case that in attributing this crime to Medea he was presenting the audience with a shockingly innovative transferral of guilt in the children's death from their enemies to the one who most should be their friend, the oppressive effect of her actions would be geometrically increased.

Euripides' buildup to the revelation that Medea will murder her children further represents a stretching of standard tragic convention. Euripides was, in fact, an early father of the dramatic technique (so normal to us today, in an era of "original" characters and plots) of deliberately and consciously heightening an audience's curiosity and sense of suspense about the eventual outcome of a plot. Such instillation in the audience of uncertainty about what direction a given story or characterization might take may be contrasted with more conventional tragic technique.[27] The classic technique for creating tension in Greek tragedy is the more static principle of tragic irony, by which the characters' ignorance of their own fates is poignantly emphasized throughout the play by the fact that the audience is perfectly aware of the story's eventual outcome; this sort of irony is predicated on the sharing of secrets between author and audience. One particularly apposite example may serve to illustrate the novelty of Euripides' technique: in Aeschylus's *Agamemnon*, it is the audience's knowledge that the play must end in death for Agamemnon and Cassandra that makes Agamemnon's capitulation to the lies and sophistries of his double-dealing wife so dramatically affecting; while Clytemnestra's onstage duplicity (lines 855ff.) is a clear prototype for Medea's, there is a very significant contrast in their effect on the audience, for Aeschylus's audience—secure in its foreknowledge of the ending dictated by received myth—is never in any doubt about Clytemnestra's motivations or ultimate intentions.

Euripides, on the other hand, destroys that understanding between author and audience, whether by deliberately rewriting (on occasion even perverting) received myth or simply by consciously inculcating doubt and suspense concerning which mythic variant he will finally adopt; in its place he arouses a suspicion that they should expect the unexpected. The dynamic dramatic tension thus produced may be contrasted with the static tension characteristic of tragic irony, since it is based on a step-by-step revelation of knowledge, through the planting of hints or clues to the eventual outcome of the plot. In place of an intensifying sense of the characters' pathetic ignorance of the road events will take them, the audience is afflicted, as its expectations are skewed now one way, now another, with a growing suspicion that, along with the characters, they themselves will be undone by the outcome of the play. The audience's shocked response to the play's actual events is thus replicated by their experience of its dramatic technique.

3

Medea as *Gunē en Gunaixin*

Thus far we have considered the dramatic techniques by which Euripides has led the audience to the stunning realization that his Medea will commit the ultimate crime of killing her own children. This twist in the plot in turn forces the audience to an abrupt reassessment of all that has come before.

I

It has often been noted by critics that in this play Euripides has chosen to downplay Medea's supernatural powers almost totally until the end of the play, when she assumes her demonic aspect and flies away in Helios's magic chariot.[1] In order to appreciate the tensions created by Medea's characterization, however, the precise admixture of the realistic and the demonic in the character must be examined in further detail, not just as a linear progression from one to the other, but as a purposely paradoxical blend from the beginning of the play onward.

Right from the start of the play, Euripides is at some pains to portray Medea not solely as a woman whose immoderate passion will drive her beyond the accepted limits of human behavior, but (right alongside that characterization, and sitting somewhat uneasily with it) as spokeswoman for the fears and pressures faced by ordinary

fifth-century Athenian wives in a male-dominated world.[2] It is clear
early on that this divorce is to proceed along the lines prescribed by
society—Euripides' and his audience's society.[3]

Even Medea—sorceress and already a double murderer—is not lib-
erated enough to imagine flying off in her magic chariot and setting
up housekeeping as a single woman.[4] Of course not, one may say;
such a thing was totally unheard of. That rejoinder would be indisput-
ably correct in respect to actual Athenian women. But the Medea of
myth is as powerful a sorceress as her demigoddess aunt Circe; even
her mortality is in question.[5] Circe lived on a deserted island, sexually
mature and dangerous, prone to acts of aggression and sexual posses-
siveness against passing male sailors. It is easier to fit the character of
Medea into that mold than it is to watch her bemoan her helplessness
(as opposed to her anger and hurt pride and sexuality: *those* seem
natural) now that Jason has divorced her. Euripides could certainly
have emphasized Medea's Circe-like qualities, if he had wanted to.
But he has chosen otherwise, and the effects of his choice will, then,
bear examination.

Athenian customs concerning divorce were simple. Once a man
decided, often unilaterally (as Jason did), that he wished a divorce, he
had only to repudiate his wife formally and send her, dowry in hand,
back to her father or other male guardian. The emotions engendered
in the woman by such a procedure may well have included at times a
more moderate degree of Medea's rage and humiliation. After all, her
marriage was all she had. But the procedure was a completely everyday one, condoned by society. The female Chorus in our play voices
resigned recognition of this fact (155–57; see below, pp. 63ff.); an
undercurrent of support for male sovereignty has been identified by
Pucci even in the Nurse's sympathetic outlining of Medea's woes in
the prologue.[6] The countervailing feature of the system is that the
woman was never left helpless and alone: that is, she was never bereft
of the male protection that Greek society deemed the *sine qua non* for
the weaker female sex. Within this system, however, Medea's case
was problematic: upon leaving Colchis with her lover in the first
place, she had defrauded her father of his most prized possession and
murdered her brother in order to delay pursuit. Thus she can scarcely
return to her father's protection, as she and others in the play point
out repeatedly.[7]

But Medea is also a foreigner, and, interestingly, this status could
have worked to her benefit (as Jason explains), εἴ σε μὴ κνίζοι λέχος: "if
the question of your bed were not griping you" (568). Here Jason as-

sumes the legal right of the fifth-century Athenian husband to marry and have children by a citizen woman, while keeping a foreign, noncitizen woman as a concubine and providing openly for her and his children by her. So Jason tells us in the long speech in which he tries to convince Medea that, if she had only remained calm and unthreatening to the royal family, her position and that of their sons would in fact be strengthened by Jason's royal alliance (see especially 559–67).[8] She has spoiled it all for herself, he says, by her sexual jealousy (569–73).

But, while Medea is in no way subservient enough to accept number-two-wife status, neither is she ready to emulate her paternal aunt's independent life on Aeaea: her plans for revenge cannot proceed until she finds Aegeus as surrogate male guardian to protect her.[9] The clash between the "resource" of the magic chariot and Medea's "need" for Aegeus as protector provides an anomaly that fanned Norwood's flames (see note 4 above). Medea the sorceress would have illimitable options open to her; Medea the wife is bound by the restraints of Euripides' society. There is no doubt that Euripides' choice to portray Medea thus as a prisoner of society was purposeful and will be revealed to have special significance to the play's intended effects on its audience.

Even beyond the confinement of Medea's options in the divorce within standard societal expectations, Medea is taken, however inappropriately, as representative of the condition of the typical Athenian housewife (or, given the Greeks' limited purview of the possible relationships between the sexes, of Woman herself). Her great entrance speech (214ff.) contains a moving manifesto:

πάντων δ' ὅσ' ἔστ' ἔμψυχα καὶ γνώμην ἔχει
γυναῖκές ἐσμεν ἀθλιώτατον φυτόν·
ἃς πρῶτα μὲν δεῖ χρημάτων ὑπερβολῇ
πόσιν πρίασθαι, δεσπότην τε σώματος
λαβεῖν· κακοῦ γὰρ τοῦτ' ἔτ' ἄλγιον κακόν.
κἀν τῷδ' ἀγὼν μέγιστος, ἢ κακὸν λαβεῖν
ἢ χρηστόν. οὐ γὰρ εὐκλεεῖς ἀπαλλαγαὶ
γυναιξίν, οὐδ' οἷόν τ' ἀνήνασθαι πόσιν.
ἐς καινὰ δ' ἤθη καὶ νόμους ἀφιγμένην
δεῖ μάντιν εἶναι, μὴ μαθοῦσαν οἴκοθεν,
ὅτῳ μάλιστα χρήσεται ξυνευνέτῃ.
κἂν μὲν τάδ' ἡμῖν ἐκπονουμέναισιν εὖ
πόσις ξυνοικῇ μὴ βίᾳ φέρων ζυγόν,
ζηλωτὸς αἰών· εἰ δὲ μή, θανεῖν χρεών.

ἀνὴρ δ᾽, ὅταν τοῖς ἔνδον ἄχθηται ξυνών,
ἔξω μολὼν ἔπαυσε καρδίαν ἄσης·

. . . .

ἡμῖν δ᾽ ἀνάγκη πρὸς μίαν ψυχὴν βλέπειν.
λέγουσι δ᾽ ἡμᾶς ὡς ἀκίνδυνον βίον
ζῶμεν κατ᾽ οἴκους, οἳ δὲ μάρνανται δορί·
κακῶς φρονοῦντες· ὡς τρὶς ἂν παρ᾽ ἀσπίδα
στῆναι θέλοιμ᾽ ἂν μᾶλλον ἢ τεκεῖν ἅπαξ.

Of all things that are alive and have sense, we women are
the most miserable breed. First we have to buy a husband
with an extravagant dowry, and so take a master over our
body—the latter evil more painful than the former. And in
this the greatest struggle is whether you take a good one or
a bad one, for divorce brings ill repute upon women, nor
can a woman spurn her husband. But coming to a new
house, with new ways and customs, she must play sooth-
sayer (though she learned no such art at home), to see how
best she may handle her bed-mate. And if we work all this
out well and our husband lives with us bearing the yoke
easily, then our life is enviable. But if not, we might as well
die. Now the man, whenever he is tired of the company at
home, can go out-of-doors and put an end to his vexation.
But as for us, we must look to a single soul alone. They talk
about living our lives danger-free at home, while they fight
with the spear. But they are wrong. I would much rather
stand three times in battle than once give birth.

(230–51)

It is well known that this characterization of the evil helplessness of
woman's lot is related to a fragment from Sophocles' *Tereus* on the
same subject:

νῦν δ᾽ οὐδέν εἰμι χωρίς. ἀλλὰ πολλάκις
ἔβλεψα ταύτῃ τὴν γυναικείαν φύσιν,
ὡς οὐδέν ἐσμεν. αἳ νέαι μὲν ἐν πατρὸς
ἥδιστον, οἶμαι, ζῶμεν ἀνθρώπων βίον·
τερπνῶς γὰρ ἀεὶ παῖδας ἄνοια τρέφει.
ὅταν δ᾽ ἐς ἥβην ἐξικώμεθ᾽ ἔμφρονες,
ὠθούμεθ᾽ ἔξω καὶ διεμπολώμεθα
θεῶν πατρῴων τῶν τε φυσάντων ἄπο,

αἳ μὲν ξένους πρὸς ἄνδρας, αἳ δὲ βαρβάρους,
αἳ δ' εἰς ἀληθῆ δώμαθ', αἳ δ' ἐπίρροθα.
καὶ ταῦτ', ἐπειδὰν εὐφρόνη ζεύξῃ μία,
χρεὼν ἐπαινεῖν καὶ δοκεῖν καλῶς ἔχειν.

Now on my own I am nothing. But I have often regarded
the female race so, that we are nothing. When we are
young we live the sweetest of mortal lives in our fathers'
homes, for children are ever supported in their content-
ment by their naïveté. But when we come of age, more
aware now, we are thrust out and sold to the highest bid-
der, away from the gods of our fathers and from our fathers themselves—some sent to foreigners, some to bar-
barians; some to true homes, others to carping ones. And
when a single night has joined the two of us, we're expected to bless our fate and consider ourselves well off.

(Fr. 524 Nauck)

Procne is quite evidently the mythic source from which the child-
murdering element has been grafted onto the character of Medea.[10]
But, whereas the crime the two women will commit is identical, there is
a distinct contrast between the two. The Athenian Procne indeed was
"sold" into submission to an unknown man, a foreigner (the Thracians
were noted for their wild and uncivilized behavior); her husband will
prove himself eminently *kakos* by raping and mutilating her sister,
while concomitantly deceiving and betraying his wife's trust. Medea,
on the other hand, is herself the foreigner; the resultant prejudice is
apparent in lines 222, 255–56, 536ff., 591–92, and 1329–43. She was not
sold, unwilling, to a suitor her father found desirable for politico-
dynastic purposes; she herself chose Jason, out of love and passion and
to the eternal regret of her father. She did bring Jason a fine dowry, the
Golden Fleece, but it was not at her father's giving. And her post-
marital murder of Pelias, well known to the audience even without
elliptical references to it at lines 9–10, 484ff., and 504–5, and the cause
of Jason's exile to Corinth in the first place, makes it particularly difficult to see her as a meek and subdued *Hausfrau*, though we may readily
grant the monogamous direction of her passion.

Any sure inferences concerning the relationship between these two
passages are precluded by the fact that the date of Sophocles' *Tereus* is
unknown.[11] Nonetheless, it is tempting to posit an earlier date for the
Tereus than for the *Medea*, on the grounds that thus we may draw a

picture of Euripides as in the process here of one of his characteristic deformations. Newton has demonstrated that the substantive and formal anomalies of the Chorus's paradigmatic likening of Medea to Ino at the end of the play have the paradoxical effect of implicitly negating the similarities between the two cases.[12] Just so, Medea's adoption as her own of topics which had recently been voiced on the Athenian stage by the Procne of Sophocles would have complex and to a certain extent contradictory effects. First of all, the passage would thus provide its own foreshadowing of the novel turn in mythic events to be taken at the end of the play when Medea murders her children—for in the end the likeness between the two women suggested here by their similar laments on the lot of the Greek wife will be hammered home by the identity of their responses to the injustice meted out to them by their husbands. Second, however, the imperfection of the parallel drawn would highlight the dissimilarities between the two women's cases and so serve to indict Medea all the more for her crimes. Thus Euripides, if the speculation that Sophocles' play preceded his own is true, may be seen to have deliberately inverted a sentiment about the grievous lot of womankind (which in its Sophoclean locus had legitimacy) by placing it instead into the mouth of a character who is signally atypical of the Athenian womanhood she here pretends to speak for.

The effects of the setting of Medea within societal confines, then, are two-edged. There is blatant contrast between Medea's adoption as her own of the common woman's plight (214ff.) and both her standard mythic characterization as an aggressive, dangerous woman and the Nurse's direct characterization of her as *deinē*: "terrible" (44) in the darkly foreboding opening scene. The further anomaly that, even as Medea laments the harm she has suffered as a wife set in necessarily passive relation to her husband, she herself adopts the language and posture of the active (and properly masculine) heroic code has been illuminated in detail elsewhere.[13] These contrasts serve to implant in the audience an uneasy sense that all may not be what it seems. Early sympathy has naturally fastened on Medea, a woman wronged by her husband, a woman whose house (in other words, her whole world) has been shattered by a callously ungrateful opportunist. The villain of the piece is clearly Jason, whose sins include not only the breaking of oaths to the wife who had saved him from numerous snares of death, but also a heartless lack of solicitude toward his own sons; Medea is joined by the more objective sources of the Nurse, the *Paidagōgos*, and the Chorus in attesting to this assessment of blame.

As Grube has put it, ". . . no one has a word to say for Jason, except himself."[14] When the grotesque nature of Medea's proposed revenge is announced, however, a radical readjustment of sympathies and expectations is forced upon the audience. As the audience undertakes this readjustment, they will necessarily be afflicted with a certain indignation: Medea, by asserting her identity with the everyday Athenian woman and, concomitantly, downplaying her supernatural qualities (which would allow her to transcend the boundaries imposed by a given societal configuration, as a purely mortal woman might not), has manipulated the audience into a false sense of both sympathy and empathy. The communality of all women has been hoisted up like a banner and used to deceive them into a false identification of Medea and Everywoman. But Medea's willing embarkation upon the crime most unspeakable to the generality of womankind utterly belies their empathy and leaves them with a sense that Medea has duped them just as hypocritically and calculatingly as she has duped Creon and Aegeus.

Nonetheless, this reversal of the audience's feelings toward Medea does not render her comments on the sociological facts of womanhood any the less valid. Although (so we discover) the helpless plight of womankind as she describes it cannot aptly be applied to her, still, at the time when the character speaks these words, she is speaking words which would surely ring realistically and affectingly among an Athenian audience. And once those sympathetic chords have been struck, some sense of the justifiability of Medea's anger at Jason must linger, despite an overlay of revulsion at the form in which she proposes to exact her revenge. Just so, the Chorus, even after they have rejected the particular form of Medea's planned revenge as loathsome and unnatural, maintains an unswervingly negative judgment concerning Jason:

> ἔοιχ' ὁ δαίμων πολλὰ τῇδ' ἐν ἡμέρᾳ
> κακὰ ξυνάπτειν ἐνδίκως Ἰάσονι.

Fortune has, it seems, on this day enmeshed Jason in many evils—and deservedly so.

(1231–32)

It would be artificial to go further and attempt to distinguish the separate reactions to this turn in the play of the hypothetical female and the hypothetical male audience member—even if one could feel completely secure in the assumption that both sexes were represented in the audience.[15] Each of us reacts to literature as *both* man and woman; our empathy is hermaphroditic; it is not limited to those of our same sex. In a play which depends so critically on the conflict first between a man and a woman and then between the distinct societal roles allotted to the two sexes, however, a certain measure of schematization may be excusable in the interest of comprehending more precisely the effects of Euripides' various techniques. Thus, let us posit for the moment an ideal "Female" response to the development in Medea's character, juxtaposed with an ideal "Male" response. Each of these "ideas" (*eidea*), of course, is real only in the abstract realm; neither can be attached to an actual human viewer or reader, for any real person's responses partake of both male and female ideals, blended in a proportion peculiar to the individual.

Indignation at Medea's duplicitous appeal to empathy is a response which would be common to both "Male" and "Female" *eidea*. However, the exact direction of the disillusionment experienced by the two would diverge. Indignant response to Medea's manipulative use of the communality of women and a resultant condemnation of Medea as an unnatural woman would afflict the "Female" more heavily. The "Male" reaction might more likely vacillate between a similar reaction to Medea as an aberrant individual and a queasy impulse to take the identification of Medea and Everywoman one step further. The reasoning behind this latter reaction would be as follows: if, as Medea asserts at lines 214ff., she is like all women, then perhaps all women (despite their disclaimers) are capable of the same abominations as Medea. Such a reaction would result in a heightened sense that heavy societal restrictions laid upon women may potentially backfire, that the subsurface smoldering that they generate may burst out into the open in destructive flashes. We know that Euripides was aware of such repercussions of repression, especially as regards women, from his great play on that theme, the *Bacchae*.[16]

In sum, as the character of Medea moves from her women's manifesto to her declaration of her unnatural intentions regarding her children, the abstractly "Female" reaction is to change from sympathy and empathy to revulsion: *I've been duped. She is not like other women after all.* The "Male" sequence of thought, on the other hand, will turn from an initial reaction of sympathy (perhaps qualified) to a terrifying glimpse of the nether regions of the woman's "true" soul: *Maybe all women are not so different from Medea after all.*

II

As the play continues after Medea's revelation of her murderous plan, perhaps the single element by which Euripides most dramatically and effectively maintains and maximizes the audience's sense of horror at her impending crime is the attribution to Medea herself of temporary failures in her resolve. Such a statement may seem paradoxical. At first blush, Medea's onrushes of normal maternal feelings might more naturally seem to make her more sympathetic, to acquit her, in a sense, of a charge of unnaturalness. To some extent, these mitigating effects do occur.[17] It is my contention, however, that the primary result of Medea's waverings is precisely the opposite: to emphasize the grotesquerie of her crime and the utter horror of her being able to carry it through.

It is at this point that one of the major purposes of Euripides' de-emphasis of Medea's supernatural qualities becomes clear. Beings who live outside the realm of human life, whether gods, demigods, or mortals with supernatural powers, naturally live beyond the bounds of human ethics as well. If Medea were a sorceress through and through, if Euripides had chosen to accentuate her nearness to the world of the immortals (to which she probably initially belonged [see note 5 above]), then her acts could somehow be viewed as outside human limits. Similarly, a totally demonic Medea—an embodiment or personification of the cosmic force of *thumos*, which Medea herself names as her motive force at line 1079—might commit the same crimes to a different effect.[18] Such a Medea would appeal to our intellects, to that part of our literary sensibility which seeks out and thrives on metaphors and allegories.[19] Since she need not in that case be judged ultimately as a human being, her "existence" in the play would not create such a sense of moral turmoil.

As it is, however, Euripides' Medea goes out of her way—in the "wavering" scenes as in her entrance speech—to give the impression that she *is* a normal woman, that she shares with other mothers all their incessant hopes and fears and plans for their young, the fruits of their *ponoi*: "labors". Thus, she sketches her now vain visions of attending her sons on the occasion of their marriages and of having them as props for her weakened old age (1024–36); thus, she makes allusion (albeit with deceitful intent) to the irrational and unspecific fearfulness of all mothers toward their children (929–31). The natural concomitant of this assertion of normalcy is, as suggested above, the implication that, conversely, normal women might undertake the same "unnatural" course as Medea. Additionally, the seesawing from firm decision to wavering irresolution serves to intensify to an almost unbearable degree the audience's tension and suspense concerning the play's outcome.[20] For it may be assumed that the audience would still be hoping against hope that Medea would relent (and further— on the presumption that they were less than fully prepared by received tradition for the deliberate child-murder—that the play might be allowed to return to a beaten mythic track). Even though, in the latter eventuality, the children were still to die (e.g., at the hands of the Corinthians), the audience would surely consider it preferable, in contradiction to Medea's words at line 1239, for the children to die δυσμενεστέρᾳ χερί: "by a more hostile hand"; after all, the hostile hand is clearly a more natural and appropriate tool for destruction than the friendly one.

Let us briefly trace the movement of the play from Medea's announcement of her plan for the children (791–93) to the arrival onstage of the Messenger reporting the princess's death and sealing the children's doom (1121ff.). After an initial reproach by the Chorus, the action turns first to a scene between Medea and Jason, in which she seeks to persuade him to intercede with his bride for the children's reprieve (866ff.). She calculatingly bases this appeal on the change of heart tender solicitude for her children's welfare has supposedly effected (οὐκ εἰσὶ μέν μοι παῖδες . . . ;: "Do I not have children?" [880]). The audience must groan at the irony: she has them now, but will not for long if she follows through with her plan. Her support of her plan by pretended concern for the very ones she intends to sacrifice to her *thumos* depicts her as utterly hypocritical and shameless; it rankles with her audience, who now know her true plans, like pressing on a bruise. It also recalls and highlights the hypocrisy of her deceitful appeal at 340ff. to Creon as fellow parent.

At line 894, she trots the children onstage for further manipulative effect on Jason. Once they appear, however, her resolve begins to crumple. Two successive episodes between Medea and Jason, predicated on a form of tragic irony (see ch. 2, n. 27) in which the double application of each sentiment contributes to an excruciating tension for the audience, end in temporary emotional breakdowns by Medea (899ff., 922ff.). Jason's so-misplaced confidence that he, as the man of the family, is the one on whom his children's future depends results in such pathos that even Medea apparently breaks down; his complacent prediction of future prosperity for his sons gives way

abruptly to his puzzlement at Medea's reaction to his comforting
words:

ὑμῖν δέ, παῖδες, οὐκ ἀφροντίστως πατὴρ
πολλὴν ἔθηκε σὺν θεοῖς σωτηρίαν·
οἶμαι γὰρ ὑμᾶς τῆσδε γῆς Κορινθίας
τὰ πρῶτ᾽ ἔσεσθαι σὺν κασιγνήτοις ἔτι.
ἀλλ᾽ αὐξάνεσθε· τἄλλα δ᾽ ἐξεργάζεται
πατήρ τε καὶ θεῶν ὅστις ἐστὶν εὐμενής·
ἴδοιμι δ᾽ ὑμᾶς εὐτραφεῖς ἥβης τέλος
μολόντας, ἐχθρῶν τῶν ἐμῶν ὑπερτέρους.
αὕτη, τί χλωροῖς δακρύοις τέγγεις κόρας,
στρέψασα λευκὴν ἔμπαλιν παρηίδα;
κοὐκ ἀσμένη τόνδ᾽ ἐξ ἐμοῦ δέχῃ λόγον;

As for you, my children, your father has arranged a great
guarantee of your safety, with the help of the gods and
with careful attention. For I think that you will be the
pinnacle of this land of Corinth, you and your brothers,
hereafter. All you must do is grow: the rest your father is
taking care of, along with whatever deity is favorable to
us. May I only see you come thriving to the prime of your
youth, mightier than my enemies.—But you, lady, why do
you wet your cheeks with fresh tears and turn your pale
cheek away? Is the manner of my speech not welcome to
you?

(914–24)

A third repetition of the now-established pattern of double entendre
followed by an emotional breakdown by Medea occurs in the inter-
change between Medea and the *Paidagōgos* (1002ff.).

The first sign of actual hesitancy on Medea's part to go through
with her plan, however, appears in her exquisitely poignant speech at
lines 1019ff. After sending the *Paidagōgos* inside to perform his daily
(and now superfluous) duties on behalf of the children,[21] Medea em-
barks on a speech which represents one of the high points in all
literature of play on an audience's emotions.

After an elegiac lament on the pleasures and dreams that will be
lost to her in the future (1021–39), the mother is abruptly recalled to
the present by the physical presence of her children, and it is now for
the first time that her resolve is truly shaken:

φεῦ φεῦ· τί προσδέρκεσθέ μ' ὄμμασιν, τέκνα;
τί προσγελᾶτε τὸν πανύστατον γέλων;
αἰαῖ· τί δράσω; καρδία γὰρ οἴχεται,
γυναῖκες, ὄμμα φαιδρὸν ὡς εἶδον τέκνων.
οὐκ ἂν δυναίμην· χαιρέτω βουλεύματα
τὰ πρόσθεν· ἄξω παῖδας ἐκ γαίας ἐμούς.
τί δεῖ με πατέρα τῶνδε τοῖς τούτων κακοῖς
λυποῦσαν αὐτὴν δὶς τόσα κτᾶσθαι κακά;
οὐ δῆτ' ἔγωγε. χαιρέτω βουλεύματα.

Alas! Why do you turn your eyes' gaze upon me, children?
Why do you laugh that final laugh? Oh god, what shall I
do? My strength is gone, women—it left when I saw my
children's shining glance. I couldn't do it. Farewell to my
previous plans—I shall take my children with me from this
land. Why, by hurting their father through their suffering,
should I have to bring twice the pain on myself? No, I
won't do it! Farewell, my plans!

(1040–48)

Her *thumos* quickly reasserts itself, however, as she veers into antici-
pation of the mockery she may incur by inaction:

καίτοι τί πάσχω; βούλομαι γέλωτ' ὀφλεῖν
ἐχθροὺς μεθεῖσα τοὺς ἐμοὺς ἀζημίους;
τολμητέον τάδ'. ἀλλὰ τῆς ἐμῆς κάκης,
τὸ καὶ προσέσθαι μαλθακοὺς λόγους φρενί.

And yet, what is the matter with me? Do I want to be a
laughing-stock for letting my enemies off unscathed? I
must do it. Oh, my cowardice, to have even admitted to
my mind such soft thoughts!

(1049–52)

These lines recall her words earlier in lines 797 (οὐ γὰρ γελᾶσθαι
τλητὸν ἐξ ἐχθρῶν, φίλαι: "for it is insupportable, friends, to be
laughed at by enemies") and 807–10:

μηδείς με φαύλην κἀσθενῆ νομιζέτω
μηδ' ἡσυχαίαν, ἀλλὰ θατέρου τρόπου,
βαρεῖαν ἐχθροῖς καὶ φίλοισιν εὐμενῆ·
τῶν γὰρ τοιούτων εὐκλεέστατος βίος.

> May no one think me poor-minded or weak, nor mild, but
> the reverse, grievous to my enemies and of benefit to my
> near and dear. For the lives of people such as this have
> best fame.

These are standard heroic sentiments, which in Euripides' time were
only beginning to be challenged as the proper philosophical basis for
the conduct of one's life.[22] There is no reason to assume that their basic
tenet would be unacceptable to more than the advanced thinkers in
Euripides' audience. The irony of their appearance here, however, is
nonetheless quite real and surely appreciable by Euripides' audience. It
rests on the fact that these standard sentiments are misapplied by
Medea (as were her claim to communality with the ordinary Athenian
housewife and her protestations against the unfair prejudice attached
to her "intelligence"). Surely the audience would not miss the ironic
inappropriateness—lost on Medea in her rush to rationalization of her
proposed crime—of Medea's specific description of herself as βαρεῖαν
ἐχθροῖς καὶ φίλοισιν εὐμενῆ: "grievous to my enemies and of benefit to
my near and dear," when her proposed means of vengeance on her
enemies integrally entails her violation of the sacred ties of family and
affection as well: the murder of her innocent children will prove her, in
sharp contrast to her self-characterization, φιλτάτοις δυσμενής: "hostile to her nearest and dearest."[23]

Beyond this contradiction, Medea's moral confusion is also reflected, again ironically, by the fact that in her delusion she feels that
it is her lapses into normal human tenderness toward her loved ones
which are base ("Oh, my cowardice!"); she ironically views her re-
newal of criminal resolve as a return to sanity or proper conduct.
Underlying this moral confusion, it is evident, is the inversion of
some basic societal definitions, on the part of both character and
author. "Grievous to my enemies and of benefit to my near and dear":
Knox and Bongie have amply demonstrated that these formulaic
words, along with her actions and her general cast of mind, set Medea
squarely within the heroic tradition (see n. 22 and Intro., n. 1); she
becomes, in Bongie's words, "in the code of the ancient heroic system, a veritable 'saint.' "[24] Yet the heroic mold was an essentially
masculine one; it was "despite her gender" that Medea "lived by the
same rules as Achilles, Ajax and other great literary heroes before
her."[25] Certainly no role could be further from that of such a hero than
the role of Everywoman so emphatically assumed by Medea at the
beginning of the play. While in pre-Euripidean tragedy a Clytemnestra or an Antigone could take on heroic stature and attitudes (and so

become, in a sense, masculinized), when they did so it was to champion an essentially female cause: the preservation of the sanctity of the family.[26] It is an ever so characteristically Euripidean deformation, first, that his heroine's ascription to the male heroic code must necessarily involve the demolition of the female and specifically maternal aspects of her; second, that he highlights starkly the anomaly between the two aspects of his protagonist's character as hero and as Everywoman; and, third, that he portrays her interior dialogue as a battle between two definitions of "virtue." The loser in the battle is the normal societal definition of female virtue, to which Medea's natural maternal instincts incline her; the winner is the masculine heroic model to which Medea aspires—but in such a distorted version that in order to achieve the half less natural for her sex (to be "grievous to [her] enemies") the woman must fail in the other, supposedly innate half (to be "of benefit to [her] near and dear").

As the action continues, Medea coldly prepares for murder by pronouncing standard ritualistic formulae to ward off unpropitious effects upon her "sacrifice" (1054).[27] But again her resolve breaks, and she enters a plea for mercy upon the children addressed directly to her *thumos*:[28]

> μὴ δῆτα, θυμέ, μὴ σύ γ᾽ ἐργάσῃ τάδε·
> ἔασον αὐτούς, ὦ τάλαν, φεῖσαι τέκνων·
> ἐκεῖ μεθ᾽ ἡμῶν ζῶντες εὐφρανοῦσί σε.

> No, my heart, I pray, do not do this. Let them go, poor wretch—spare the children. They will give you joy if they live there [sc., in Athens] with us.

> (1056–58)

While the address to one's heart was a commonplace in early Greek literature, the *thumos* which Medea addresses here is not simply a synonym for *kardia*, as it is in other such addresses.[29] No English translation can capture the full effect of the double application of the Greek word *thumos* to both the emotion (passionate anger) and its seat, the heart; but clearly both meanings are at work here, as the subsequent use of *thumos* for overwhelming anger (1079) confirms. Furthermore, the precise phrasing of this address clarifies the pathological state of Medea's mind. She is so far out of control that she views her *thumos* as having a life of its own, *outside* and *in conflict with* herself.[30] This split between her selves is reflected both by the emphatic *su:* "you" of line 1056 and by her use of both second-person and first-person pronouns in line 1058: "You, my heart (*thume, su*)—spare them, for if they live with me/us (*meth' hēmōn*) in Athens they will cheer you (*se*)."[31] Her final tightening of resolve is based on a self-serving delusion (anticipating lines 1238–40) that, if she does not kill the children, they will necessarily die at the hands of the Corinthians. I have used the word "delusion" since Medea's assumption is clearly not logical within the dramatic framework of the play: not only is it inconsistent with the earlier-voiced possibility that she might take them with her to Athens (1045, 1058), but in the end Medea will carry her sons' dead bodies away to the temple of Hera Acraea in the magic chariot; surely she could just as easily have taken them with her alive, thus saving them from the Corinthians' wrath.[32] Her lack of logic has suitably been taken to reflect the confusion of her mind and is, as Page has noted, "intensely moving and dramatic: emendation or dele-tion destroys all the force of Medea's changes of temper."[33] In this view, Page represents one side of a continuing critical polemic. The opposite view is presented by Kovacs:

> Excision [of lines 1056–80, as first proposed by Bergk in 1884 and recently adopted by James Diggle in his new text of Euripides (Oxford, 1984)] disembarrasses us of a Medea who argues to herself (1051–61) "I'll not kill the children but take them to Athens. But no, I must kill them because otherwise I will be leaving them to suffer outrage from the Corinthians." Such an argument is nonsense, and those who attempt to justify it by reference to Medea's supposed state of mind would do well, as Reeve says, to "favour the sceptical . . . with a demonstration that calculated illogi-cality was a recognized device in ancient poetry; or were the poets themselves thrown off balance by the emotion of their characters?" (p. 57 n. 11). No measures to eliminate this absurdity less drastic than excision of 1056–80 have thus far succeeded.[34]

As one of those lectured here by Kovacs and Reeve for subscribing to and condoning nonsense, this critic remains (as often) stolidly un-concerned by a piece of poetic illogic which has plagued others. Psy-chologically, Page's assessment is more insightful than his oppo-nents' plea for logic; beyond the level of dramatic characterization, far

from having been sympathetically "thrown off balance" by his heroine's emotions, Euripides has taken the opportunity presented by
Medea's distraction to present the audience with another instance of
the kind of authorial cleverness which is more and more coming to be
seen as characteristic of his artistry.

To wit, in putting patent illogicalities into his character's mouth
here, Euripides is playing a sort of double game with received myth.
Despite the speciousness of her train of thought, Medea's assumption
that the children must die *is* valid in an offbeat sense, given the
mythic traditions. Πάντως σφ' ἀνάγκη κατθανεῖν: "it is altogether
necessary that they die," she says (1240). To one who might legitimately ask, "Why?," the implicit answer is: "Because, if we don't
follow a mythic tradition in which Medea causes their death (whether
unwittingly or not), then we'll have to revert to the one where the
Corinthians do—for we know full well from myth and from the cult at
Corinth that they *do* die." In effect, the playwright has subtly broken
the bonds of dramatic convention again, to point to the children's fate
as known anachronistically to himself and his audience, though not to
the character who speaks these lines. The device is akin to the "But
where are the Messengers?" witticism identified by Winnington-
Ingram and to the subtle allusions to the playwright's own mythic
innovation which I have suggested above.[35]

The climax of Medea's speech comes with her final address directly
to the children. Just as the initial weakening of her resolve is brought
on by a look in her children's eyes and by their laughter, so the
intensely pathetic quality of this address is achieved by its continual
reference to the children's physical presence. Medea is not only speaking, she is drinking her children with her eyes, touching them, even
smelling them. Through her words, their childish beauty assaults the
audience's senses as well, bringing to mind vivid images of the exqui-
site softness and purity of small children:

> . . . δότ', ὦ τέκνα,
> δότ' ἀσπάσασθαι μητρὶ δεξιὰν χέρα.
> ὦ φιλτάτη χείρ, φίλτατον δέ μοι στόμα
> καὶ σχῆμα καὶ πρόσωπον εὐγενὲς τέκνων,
> εὐδαιμονοῖτον, ἀλλ' ἐκεῖ· τὰ δ' ἐνθάδε
> πατὴρ ἀφείλετ'. ὦ γλυκεῖα προσβολή,
> ὦ μαλθακὸς χρὼς πνεῦμά θ' ἥδιστον τέκνων.
> χωρεῖτε χωρεῖτ'· οὐκέτ' εἰμὶ προσβλέπειν
> οἶά τε †πρὸς ὑμᾶς†, ἀλλὰ νικῶμαι κακοῖς.

O children, give your mother your right hand to kiss. O dearest hand, lips dearest to me and noble face and figure of my children, may you be happy, but in a different place. What is here your father has taken away. O dear embrace! How soft the skin of children, how sweet their breath. Go away—go. I am no longer able to look upon you. I am overcome by my ills.

(1069–77)

The final three lines of Medea's speech fall on us quietly, as dénouement. Gone, temporarily, are her madness and self-delusion. For a brief moment she sees with weary clarity, almost objectively, as from outside herself:

καὶ μανθάνω μὲν οἷα δρᾶν μέλλω κακά,
θυμὸς δὲ κρείσσων τῶν ἐμῶν βουλευμάτων,
ὅσπερ μεγίστων αἴτιος κακῶν βροτοῖς.

Indeed I know what ills I am about to do, but rage is winner over my deliberations—rage, which brings the greatest ills to men.

(1078–80)

With these lines, so calm and resigned in tone, we know finally that the children are doomed to die by their mother's hand. It is the words' very lack of heat that convinces. In this uncharacteristic moment of insight, Medea sounds a theme that will recur in later plays of Euripides, that the forces that drive one to sin and self-destruction are beyond human control;[36] thus Phaedra muses:

καί μοι δοκοῦσιν οὐ κατὰ γνώμης φύσιν
πράσσειν κάκιον· ἔστι γὰρ τό γ' εὖ φρονεῖν
πολλοῖσιν· ἀλλὰ τῇδ' ἀθρητέον τόδε·
τὰ χρήστ' ἐπιστάμεσθα καὶ γιγνώσκομεν,
οὐκ ἐκπονοῦμεν δ'. . . .

It seems to me that people fare worse than is merited by the quality of their judgment, for there are many who think rightly. But here is the point: we are well acquainted with the good, we recognize it—but we cannot bring it to fruition.

(*Hipp.* 377–81)

It is partially a sense that Medea is in these few lines speaking for the playwright that makes this prediction of the play's outcome so convincing and conclusive.

The net effect of the entire wavering scene is complex. Its impact directly on the audience is both to overcome them with its pathos and to raise their tension to a fever pitch. Its effect on their perception of Medea's character is twofold: it inspires an empathetic pity for her, for the suffering she (like any mother) will clearly feel when bereft of the children she bore, at the same time as, conflictingly, it engenders in them a wild disbelief and then outrage that she (*unlike* any other mother) will be able to sacrifice her younglings, merely to render her vengeance on their father more nastily apropos than the "simple" plan announced at lines 374–75.

III

In addition to working on his audience directly through aspects of Medea's character and actions, Euripides also enhances the terrible quality of Medea's crime by filtering it through the moral sensibility of the Chorus. The choruses of Greek drama cannot generally be said to speak for their playwrights. The sentiments they express are often too ordinary, too pat and even banal to be credited with mirroring the intricate and complex worldviews of the gifted creative minds behind these plays. They have, of course, a large and essential dramatic function, whose pursuit has both led critics into acrimonious dispute and drawn from them noble and sincere attempts to delineate in words an overriding generalization concerning this critical component of tragedy.[37] In the face of their efforts, one humble assertion may be hazarded: that one thing which the chorus can often be assumed to reflect is the more literal-minded, unoriginal, and often questionable opinions, on both philosophical and moral questions, characteristic of fifth-century Athenians. Thus, in this play, the Chorus's reactions to the protagonists may be assumed to be generally reflective of "normal" human reaction, as Euripides conceived it.[38]

Of course, one should not gloss over the fact that the Chorus is made up of women and so will reflect more precisely one-half of normal human reaction to the protagonists (as imagined by a male playwright). Furthermore, a play like the *Medea*, predicated on a

male-female conflict, will have a natural tendency to greater fac-
tionalization than a gender-neutral plot—at least initially. It is, after
all, the Chorus's granting of its allegiance to Medea as a fellow
woman, instead of to their own king and his house, that has inspired
much of the critical unease referred to in note 38. But once Medea
announces her plan to murder her children, she passes beyond normal male-female conflict; she passes, in fact, beyond the realm of
everyday humanity. As she does, the Chorus passes from a gender-
oriented complicity with Medea to revulsion against her, born of common humanity.[39]

The Chorus has no basic objection to vengeance, and they agree that
Jason's "crimes" of divorce and breach of oaths deserve it: δράσω τάδ' ·
ἐνδίκως γὰρ ἐκτείσῃ πόσιν: "I shall do as you ask, for it will be with
right that you avenge yourself upon your husband" (267), they conclude, as they agree to an oath of silence. Even when Medea includes
the princess and Creon in her revenge as well, their sympathies remain
steady.[40] To them, Creon and Creusa are properly numbered among
Medea's *echthroi*, who should not be allowed to prosper during her
misfortune. Returning to the question of Jason's dishonorable behavior, they sing an ode on the loss of respect for oaths (410ff.), imputing
the blame—in controversion of the traditional stereotypes—to *men*:

ἄνω ποταμῶν ἱερῶν χωροῦσι παγαί,
καὶ δίκα καὶ πάντα πάλιν στρέφεται.
ἀνδράσι μὲν δόλιαι βουλαί, θεῶν δ'
οὐκέτι πίστις ἄραρε.

The streams of the sacred rivers flow uphill; the proper
order of things is turned totally around. It is *men*'s coun-
sels which are treacherous; their pledges by the gods
which stay not fast.

(410–13)

Later, as soon as Medea has proclaimed the truth, that the instru-
ment of her vengeance will be sacrifice of her children, the Chorus's
approval turns to repugnance. Calling upon the *nomoi brotōn*: "laws of
humankind" (812), they plead with Medea to drop her plan; it is at
this point that they sing their magnificent ode (824ff., discussed in
more detail below, pp. 105ff.), asserting that the glorious and pure
city of Athens will be fouled by pollution if it receives Medea, τὰν οὐχ
ὁσίαν μετ' ἄλλων: "the one impure amid others" (850). The descrip-

tion of Athens here as ἱερῶν ποταμῶν / . . . πόλις: "city of sacred rivers" (846–47) clearly recalls the beginning of the chorus at lines 410ff. This echo of an earlier ode in which they were still convinced that Medea's story would end with better fame for women than heretofore poignantly highlights their disillusionment.[41] Their earlier confidence (410–13) has proved misplaced; Medea has taken the palm for deceitfulness. Her crimes will ultimately serve not to erase, but to intensify the δυσκέλαδος φάμα: "evil-sounding story" which traditionally attaches to womankind (420).

The most intriguing locus for the Chorus's eventual attitude toward Medea, however, is the ode at lines 1081ff. This ode follows immediately upon the speech (1021ff., discussed above) in which Medea's vacillation back and forth from pity for her children to steely resolve to murder them ends with her weary conclusion that, despite better and more reasonable inclinations, her anger will win out. As Medea exits to the palace, the Chorus undertakes a reflective ode on the subject of the parent-child tie. In an elaborate prelude (1081–89), they first make it clear that they have taxed their brains to the utmost in order to puzzle through a very important question. We are now to be graced with the conclusions of their mental labors. But when these conclusions are voiced, we are left feeling somewhat at a loss, for these choral musings are somehow inappropriate, off-the-point.

It is clearly this chorus which the outspoken Norwood has most signally in mind when he condemns these "superfluous ladies" for having nothing of more import to contribute than a "twittering of 'Lackaday' and 'Who would be a parent?' "[42] For, instead of dealing directly with the problem that faces them, that the just-departed Medea proposes imminently to commit premeditated murder of her children, the Chorus rambles off into a prolonged catalogue of the various worries inflicted by children on their all-concerned parents:

> οἷσι δὲ τέκνων ἔστιν ἐν οἴκοις
> γλυκερὸν †βλάστημ᾽, ὁρῶ† μελέτῃ
> κατατρυχομένους τὸν ἅπαντα χρόνον.

> I see that those whose houses are graced by a sweet sprouting of children are worn down by care through all time.

> (1098–1100)

The ultimate trial (λύπην ἀνιαροτάτην: "most grievous pain" [1113]), they say, is that, by an evil chance (εἰ δὲ κυρῆσαι / δαίμων οὕτως: "if their luck (*daimōn*) should so turn out" [1109–10]), their children may predecease them.

The ode is a distinctly affecting one, but its relevance to the situation at hand is obscure. Medea will be predeceased by her children, but by her own will, not the vagaries of fortune. For Medea's children it is not a question (as it is in the ode) of whether their parents will manage to eke out a meager existence for them (1101–2, 1107); nor is there need to wonder whether they will turn out *chrēstoi:* "worthy" once grown to young manhood (1103–4, 1108–9). What, then, impels the Chorus to these misplaced ponderings? It is my contention that Euripides deliberately sends the Chorus on a tangent here, in order to accentuate the play's pathos and intensify the audience's horror at Medea's impending crime. The Chorus's normal parental worries are set by this ode in pointed contrast with Medea's unnatural proposal to use her children as tools for vengeance against Jason. By highlighting the contrast of Medea's purposeful plan to end her sons' lives with the normal parent's fear of his or her child's premature death as the ultimate misfortune, Euripides is quite deliberately plucking at the audience's heartstrings.

The Chorus's embarkation upon inappropriate musings on everyday parental concerns at a time when they might more suitably be confronting the subject of Medea's grim intentions further leaves the impression that the Chorus cannot fully comprehend (and indeed prefers to retreat from) the enormity of Medea's proposed action. In the interests, then, of both "understanding" it and at the same time repressing it, they translate it into more readily comprehensible terms. The pain which Medea has just predicted for herself, when she shall be bereft of her children, they imagine for themselves. They do so from an impulse toward empathy, but in this case such empathy can only be achieved by a radical alteration in the factual details leading to the state of bereavement: since the Chorus cannot imagine sharing in Medea's crime, they can only share in her suffering by transposing it into more familar terms—that is, the untimely loss of a child through disease.

One final point may be made concerning the Chorus. As previously mentioned (see page 44), they counsel Medea early on in the play to resigned acceptance of her rejection by her husband:

εἰ δὲ σὸς πόσις
καινὰ λέχη σεβίζει,
κείνῳ τόδε· μὴ χαράσσου·

Ζεύς σοι τάδε συνδικήσει . . .[43]

If your husband honors a new bed, this is his prerogative—
do not chafe. Zeus will be your advocate in this.

(155–58)

In these lines, the Chorus speaks for the "system." The sexual double
standard is viewed as an incontrovertible fact of life, and Medea is
enjoined to refrain from vain agitation against it. Such passive acquies-
cence would surely be applauded by the typically cavalier fifth-
century Athenian male; the Chorus, he would think, is exhibiting the
most laudable feminine subservience here. Even if their statement
that Zeus will be Medea's ally in this matter shows that they consider
the system somehow wrong, the vague and far-distant nature of the
recompense they foresee makes it clear that (as so often in repressed
elements of society) their "rebellious" side is satisfied by the adoption
of an attitude of martyrdom.[44] It must, then, have come to the men in
the audience as something of a blunt shock to find this Chorus of
ordinary, properly passive women falling so unquestioningly, only a
hundred lines later, into complicity with Medea's proposed revenge
against the husband whom they here acquit of any excessive wrongdo-
ing. The creepy note that there is a Medea lurking in every woman is
again struck.

4

Kai ta dokēthent' ouk etelesthē

A characterizing element of Euripidean artistry is a flat refusal to let
his audience fall into an easy (and to them probably desirable) distinction of good and bad in moral situations. Page says: "He does not
condemn; he does not even criticize." Not openly enough, at any rate,
that the audience may be sure what moral judgment he, as playwright, is making. But neither does he condone. Page goes on to
characterize Euripides' moral posture by saying first, "He tries to
understand," and later, ". . . what is the poet's purpose? It is to reveal in general what human nature really is or may be. . . ."[1] But this
picture of Euripides as an objective and realistic observer of human
nature is not sufficient to explain the moral turmoil his play creates.
Yes, he is a faithful recorder of psychological phenomena and dynamics. But that is not all he is. His characters are the way they are and do
the things they do, and are juxtaposed with other characters and set
in particular situations, to a particular point and purpose. The *aporia*
of the audience member who would make moral judgments results
from the fact that much of that point and purpose is to render such
judgments meaningless. A specific technique by which the playwright achieves this end is to seem to be leading us in one direction,
then not only to slip off on a different track, but also to expose us as
naïve for having relied on his first set of signals, now revealed as
false. He weaves to unweave.

I

Page captures masterfully the movement of the audience's sympathies and moral judgments in the *Medea:*

> All this is unedifying, even sordid. Half-way through the play our sympathies are decidedly with Medea. The story, unpleasant and unheroic as it is in theme and treatment, is at least moving naturally toward an acceptable conclusion. There are many ways in which the wrath of Heaven may fall on Jason, and justice may be done. But then Medea confounds our expectations through the appalling revenge which she plans and executes. We may disapprove Jason's behaviour, but obviously his punishment is out of all proportion to his offence. At the end of the play we feel much sympathy for Jason, almost as for an innocent man overcome by dreadful calamity. Medea's vengeance is so much more criminal than the crime which it was visiting. We are watching the conquest of evil not by virtue or divine justice but by greater evil.[2]

As the play progresses, it becomes clear that nothing which seemed true at the beginning is true. Medea is not a helpless victim; she is a victimizer. She is not the protectress of her family; she is its worst enemy. When the play opens with a Medea crying out against the husband who has violated the sanctity of their family, it raises in the audience an expectation that this play will be centered on an antinomy which had become a standard one in Greek tragedy. It has already been noted that in the conventional Athenian view the woman's appointed role, both societally and biologically, was as protectress of the household.[3] This societal "given" led to a complex literary construct in which "Male" and "Female" were set in mutual antithesis. Among extant plays, for example, both Aeschylus's *Eumenides* and Sophocles' *Antigone* portray the Female as instinctive champion of the primacy of the blood-tie and of the venerable position of the family as the paramount social unit. On the other side, the Male, by a simple metaphorical leap, was taken as symbolic of a rational primary allegiance to law and state. Medea's outrage at Jason's betrayal of the family in order to ally himself with the king of Corinth (a pragmatic politico-dynastic move, and one of a type regularly made in that era through a prudent choice of marriage) initially suggests that some such male/female, family/state conflict may prove to be at the heart of this play. When Jason comes onstage, however, he champions no opposite principle. Although he clearly fancies himself as the picture of rationality in contrast with Medea's unreasoning passion, and although he names politico-dynastic purposes as his motive force at lines 547ff., he can hardly be said to "stand for" anything except a petty pragmatism; his rationality is merely slick rationalization.[4] When Medea then proceeds to "protect" the family by destroying it, root and branch, this presentation of the Female as final destroyer of the institution she so values and traditionally symbolizes is a stroke of nihilistic genius on Euripides' part.

The inversion is underlined not only by the play's action, but also by certain specific verbal reversals. At the outset of the play the *Paidagōgos* accuses Jason of selfish abandonment of proper parental concern for his children in favor of the gratification of his own libidinal urges: εἰ τούσδε γ' εὐνῆς οὕνεκ' οὐ στέργει πατήρ: "if for the sake of his bed (*eunēs*) the father fails to cherish these boys" (88). By the end of the play, the same charge can even more legitimately be cast at Medea: εὐνῆς ἕκατι καὶ λέχους σφ' ἀπώλεσας: "for the sake of your bed (*eunēs*) and your marriage you have destroyed them" (1338), says Jason (cp. line 1367). An early mention of Medea's wrath compares it to that of a lioness fiercely protecting her cubs (καίτοι τοκάδος δέργμα λεαίνης / ἀποταυροῦται δμωσίν: "and yet she rages at the servants, her savage glance that of a lioness with cubs" [187–88]); that image, which resonates oddly even at the time, for it is situated in the midst of a series of dark foreshadowings of the children's role in their mother's revenge, undergoes total ironic inversion in Jason's late descriptions of Medea, first as λέαιναν, οὐ γυναῖκα: "a lioness, not a woman" (1342), then—in an even more pointed reversal of the initial image—as παιδοφόνου τῆσδε λεαίνης: "this child-murdering lioness" (1407).

Audience perception of the character of Jason, on the other hand, is ameliorated at the play's end, even beyond the sense noted by Page that the punishment has far exceeded the crime. Jason is revealed as not so shabbily unfeeling toward his sons as the assessments of Medea, the Nurse, and the *Paidagōgos* and his own shallowly unconvincing rationalizations have made him seem. After the deaths of Creon and the princess, his first thought is to save his sons from the Corinthians' ire (1303). His discovery that they are already dead at their mother's hands inspires from him a touching grief. Medea may still dispute his care for the children (Ια. ὦ τέκνα φίλτατα. Μη. μητρί γε, σοὶ δ' οὔ: "[Ja.] O my dearest children! [Me.] Dear, yes—to their mother, not to you" [1397]); the audience, however, is now brought to the realization that it is not just for the nonperpetuation of his family line that Jason grieves, but for sons he truly loved.[5] Just as was the case in Medea's "wavering scene," it is the father's concentration on physical details that convinces us that this is no abstract pain he is feeling, but a much more concrete deprivation:

ὤμοι, φιλίου χρήζω στόματος
παίδων ὁ τάλας προσπτύξασθαι.

Alas, wretch that I am, I long to kiss my son's dear lips.

(1399–1400)

And again:

. . . δός μοι πρὸς θεῶν
μαλακοῦ χρωτὸς ψαῦσαι τέκνων.

By the gods, grant that I may touch my boys' soft skin.

(1402–3)

In his final speech he again sounds the same note of urgency for a final physical contact with his sons:

τέκνα κτείνασ' ἀποκωλύεις
ψαῦσαί τε χεροῖν θάψαι τε νεκρούς.

After killing my sons, you keep me from touching them with my hands or burying their bodies.

(1411–12)

Pointedly, Jason's reference points in these passages are the same as Medea's just before she killed the boys: each calls upon the children's lips and skin (*stoma*: cp. 1399 with 1071; *chrōs*: cp. *malakou chrōtos* [1403] with *malthakos chrōs* [1075]); and whereas Medea at lines 1069ff. grasps the boys' hands in hers (*chera* [1070], *cheir* [1071]),

Jason feels acutely the deprivation of that final touch (*psausai . . . cheroin* [1412]). Each of them loves the children, according to his or her own capacities. Yet each betrays them. Ἄρτι γιγνώσκεις τόδε, ὡς πᾶς τις αὑτὸν τοῦ πέλας μᾶλλον φιλεῖ;: "Have you only now come to realize that everyone loves himself more than his neighbor?" (85–86). The two together are responsible for their children's destruction, though each continues, in self-blindness, to attribute all blame to the other:

> Ια. ὦ τέκνα, μητρὸς ὡς κακῆς ἐκύρσατε.
> Μη. ὦ παῖδες, ὡς ὤλεσθε πατρῴα νόσῳ.

> Ja. O children, how evil the mother you have lit upon!
> Me. My sons, how you have perished because of your father's disease!

> (1363–64)

Jason exits with a wish that he had never begotten these boys to such a sorry fate:

> οὓς μήποτ' ἐγὼ φύσας ὄφελον
> πρὸς σοῦ φθιμένους ἐπιδέσθαι.

> Would that I had never begotten them, to see them killed by you.

> (1413–14)

This sentiment recalls the Chorus's earlier words on the pains of parenthood and the benefits of childlessness (1090–97). But the terms on which the speculation is predicated have been inverted here, to bitter effect. In these children's case, the question is not of the heart-consuming care children inflict on parents, but of the sufferings visited upon innocent children by parents whose care is most intensely centered upon themselves.

The reversals which have ameliorated Jason's characterization arouse an unexpected pity for him; in fact, such pity is not only unexpected but in large measure inappropriate in a play which falls into the general mold of the revenge plot. Burnett, in discussing the *Medea* as a tragedy of revenge, pinpoints several omissions or defiant reversals by Euripides of the ameliorations traditionally available within the genre, by which the vengeful protagonist's overt guilt might be mitigated.[6] It is further notable, however, that what Euripides does ameliorate at the end of the play is, in sharp contrast, the *victim's* character. This focus on the victim's suffering serves conversely to aggravate the criminality of the avenger's actions. Burnett, in speaking of a motif which appears on occasion in revenge plays, that of counterintrigue by the proposed victim, comments:

> Once allowed to behave like a principal he [the victim] would become far too interesting in himself, and if in consequence he drew the concentration of the drama to his own final *pathos*, then the play would shift from being one about doing to being one about suffering, making punishment tragedy out of its tale of revenge.[7]

It is precisely this kind of a shift which is achieved at the end of the *Medea* by the final ascription to Jason of some of the tender paternal feelings he has so scrupulously been denied previously. The pity thus unexpectedly engendered on his behalf joins the other elements of plot and form identified by Burnett in effecting a purposeful and anomalous dislocation of this plot from the conventional revenge plot.[8]

Nonetheless, this late-born pity for Jason is not sufficient to free him from the weight of the negative characterization fastened on him from the beginning of the play. He may be more sympathetic, but he is not good, nor even grand. The net effect is less to fix approbation on Jason than to detach it from Medea and, in so doing, to confound the audience's judgments. For at the same time as the playwright belies their early sense that Medea is the character who will provoke the empathy which lies at the heart of the audience's tragic experience, they are prevented from a wholehearted transferral of their allegiance to her antagonist by his own patent deficiencies of effective paternal solicitude, of the strength of character and will which would stamp him (like his wife) in the heroic mold, and finally of any thematic or symbolic weight. The audience's sympathies can attach themselves wholly to neither party; like the shades of unburied souls, they must hover disembodied, vainly seeking a final resting place.

What seemed to be has proven false; what seemed not to be is. But in place of the truths we have lost, no new truth is revealed. There is much wrong in this play, but no right. Euripides has succeeded in achieving moral chaos.

II

The nihilism of the play's outcome may be further illuminated by another critical approach. Beyond a normal human desire for compromise, such as that repeatedly voiced in Greek tragedy by proponents of *sōphrosunē* (in the *Medea*, see, e.g., lines 119–30, 635–36), there is a quasi-structural craving for mediation in a drama predicated on conflict between two protagonists and two sets of values. By partial analogy with the Lévi-Straussian view that the necessity to mediate, or soften, contradictions lies at the heart of the mythopoeic impulse, one may assert that the "ideal," or most satisfying, resolution to a drama which is born from such a polarity is one which allows of some eventual mitigation of the conflict, brought about by a mediator who is in some sense a halfway point between combatants. Such mitigation may occur either within the plot or outside it. In the former case, some form of compromise is achieved among characters who have been locked in opposition; such is the resolution of Aeschylus's *Eumenides*, as will be seen below. In the latter case, the proffered mediation is not allowed to effect any degree of rapprochement among opposed characters, but the events of the play as cast by the playwright assist the audience to their own mediation of the oppositions at the heart of the play; such will prove the case in Sophocles' *Antigone*.

In the saga of the House of Atreus as set forth by Aeschylus, a morally chaotic situation in which generation after generation is locked into an unending spiral of outrage and revenge is finally resolved through mediation, resulting in the achievement of a new order. The two sets of combatants array themselves at a unique trial scene set in the Athenian Areopagus: on the one side, the Female contingent, standing for blood-ties and natural law and including Clytemnestra and the pre-Olympian Furies; on the Male side, representing the supremacy of man-made law and societal configurations, Orestes, championed by Apollo and the other Olympian deities. The mediator is Athena, chosen as a halfway point between the sexes, because, while she is female, she has more affinities with the male sex, having been born from Zeus without benefit of a mother. This choice of Athena, it may be noted, is somewhat arbitrary, being based on accidents of her divine *persona* and a patriotic impulse to stage the trial in Athens, rather than on any intrinsic role played by the goddess within the narrative of the House of Atreus saga. Athena mediates the conflict between the male and female value systems, effecting an acceptable compromise: Apollo wins the case, but the Furies are given eternal secondary honors in a home under the earth. In its explicit resolution of the conflicts within the trilogy and its concomitant achievement of order out of chaos, the *Eumenides* is, at its end, exceptionally univocal: the audience, along with the characters, is pushed to acceptance of the mediated solution as the "correct" one, the one sanctioned by the playwright.

Mediation also occurs in Sophocles' *Antigone*, though in a somewhat less clear-cut fashion. A conflict is established between the female and male protagonists which is emblematic as well of greater conflicts, among them that of natural and man-made law and that between the individual's drive to forthright and nonconformist self-expression and her constraining society, which thrives on its members' unquestioning obedience. In this case, a mediator arises naturally from the realm of the narrative itself: Haemon, son of the king and fiancé of the king's antagonist, who agrees with his father's assertion of the necessity of *eukosmia* in the running of society but thinks this value inappropriately applied in Antigone's case. Haemon is a kind of halfway point and a point of potential linkage between the two antagonists, for his intended marriage, if it should come to pass, would doubly join Creon and Antigone (who are, of course, already related) into a single family unit; he is thus an especially suitable mediator of their conflict. The unutterably tragic ending of the play results from the fact that the mediation first attempted by Haemon is successful too late for happiness for any of the principals. Creon is impelled to defer to his son's mediation only by dire prophecies from the prophet Tiresias (who becomes, thereby, a second mediator).[9] By then, Antigone is dead; Haemon's and his mother's suicides follow soon thereafter, leaving Creon broken and ruined, to concede the virtues of the offered mediation.

The mediation within the *Antigone* is more obscure than that in the *Eumenides*, first, because of its lack of success and, second, because the meaning to be drawn from the outcome of the play is not specifically pointed by the playwright (as it had been in the *Eumenides*) but is left to the audience to assess. Critics will continue to differ as to the respective merits of Antigone's and Creon's cases, the degree to which Creon changes through suffering, and the extent to which Antigone's martyrdom gains victory for her cause, if not for her. But whatever one's answer to these and other central questions posed by the play, it is still evident that Creon's *peripeteia* at the end of the play was a direct result of his failure to compromise, to heed in timely fashion the mediation offered serially by Haemon and Tiresias. Thus the playwright guides the audience, in its own search for meaning, to a judgment weighted at least in some measure toward the values espoused by Antigone.

The moral chaos engendered by the conclusion of Euripides' *Medea* may illuminatingly be analyzed in these terms. Euripides totally defeats his audience's normal moral expectation of an eventual soothing of the conflict within the play, either through some final move to the center by one or both of the antagonists or through implicit authorial guidance of the audience to their own personal mediation of the conflicts at the heart of the play. The children born jointly of Jason and Medea would seem natural agents for such a mediation, as Haemon had been, and the clear emphasis on them in the opening scenes of the play may suggest that they will play such a role. It should be stressed, of course, that this sort of mediation need not lead to a happy ending. In keeping with the pattern of foreshadowing established early in the play, they might, for example, bring their parents toward the center only in common grief at their death: *pathei mathos*. But not only are Jason and Medea's children not allowed to soften their parents' conflict, but, with Euripides' grim touch for deformation, they become the very instruments of Medea's revenge—a wedge to drive the husband and wife more irreconcilably apart. And clearly neither protagonist learns by suffering: their continued recriminations as the play closes make that clear. The audience is left with a bleak sense that even to hope for such rapprochements is childishly unrealistic.[10] Nor is the audience to be guided to a sense of what would or could have been a proper mediation between the two antagonists, for the play's artistry is resolutely keyed not only away from solution of conflict but also toward denial of any meaning to that conflict. To side with Orestes or the Furies in the *Eumenides* or to side with Creon or Antigone in the *Antigone* involves embroilment in a complex of discords—personal, social, familial, and civic—traditionally evoked by the conflict between the sexes. By contrast, to side with either Medea or Jason at the end of Euripides' play is merely to side with one unsavory character locked in bitter and irremediable dissension with another.

It is in the play's nature, as Murray has said, that it is "painfully unsatisfying." Murray speaks for the general audience when he goes on:

> At the close of the *Medea* I actually find myself longing for a *deus ex machina*, for some being like Artemis in the

Hippolytus or the good Dioscuri of the *Electra*, to speak a
word of explanation or forgiveness, or at least leave some
sound of music in our ears to drown that dreadful and
insistent clamour of hate.[11]

Aeschylus's *Agamemnon* ends with a similar "insistent clamour of
hate," as Aegisthus and the Chorus trade carping jabs. But the *Agamemnon* is the first play of a trilogy whose final entry closes with the
achievement of compromise through mediation. In musing on the
"painfully unsatisfying" finish of the *Medea*, we may with some point
envision Euripides in a purposeful contradiction of the hopeful
worldview presented by Aeschylus and emphasized by the form of
trilogy. Imagine an *Agamemnon* with no sequel; such is the *Medea*.

III

In the wavering scene, as Medea resteels herself to her intent to
murder her children after a first onslaught of weakness, she speaks
the following words:

χωρεῖτε, παῖδες, ἐς δόμους. ὅτῳ δὲ μὴ
θέμις παρεῖναι τοῖς ἐμοῖσι θύμασιν,
αὐτῷ μελήσει· χεῖρα δ' οὐ διαφθερῶ.

Go into the house, children. And whoever lawfully may
not be present at my sacrifices, he will look to it. But I shall
not slacken my hand.

(1053–55)

These three brief lines, in which the mother evokes a sacrificial context for her slaughter of her children, have been the focus of significant critical attention. Whereas Page styles Medea's choice of words
"simply a macabre metaphor," rather than a means by which the
character "divest[s] herself of personal responsibility" for the killing,[12]
Burkert retorts: "Mere metaphor?," and, after outlining the details of
the cult of Hera Acraea, sums up, "At all events, the metaphor of the
θῦμα at the climax of Euripides' play leads back to a sacrificial ritual
which comprises the mystery of death."[13] Most recently, Pucci has
wedded these two views, accepting Burkert's opinion that Medea's
choice of words reflects the role of the Corinthian ritual as the *aition*

for the children's murder but analyzing the words in detail as a meta-phor. This metaphor in turn becomes a centerpiece of Pucci's thesis that Euripides' artistic intent may be viewed as parallel to the purifica-tory and remedial force of the sacrifice it is based upon.[14]

This study will approach the sacrificial metaphor from a different perspective, to assert that the issuance of this metaphor from the lips of a mother who will imminently slay her children serves to evoke for the audience the larger mythic and tragic context within which par-ents sacrifice their children, most signally the sacrifice of Iphigenia by her father, Agamemnon.[15] That analogy with the slaying of Iphigenia was implied by Medea's adoption of a sacrificial metaphor here is especially likely in the context of the instances of implicit comparison with Aeschylus's *Oresteia* which have already been discussed.

The work of scholars concerned with the relationship between sacri-fice and drama has suggested that the presentation of a sacrifice in a tragedy provides the author with a platform from which to address issues of a cosmic nature. As Foley has summarized:

> In sum, sacrificial procedure offers to the poet a kind of grammar of procedural terms by which to articulate in a compressed and symbolic form the nature of the relations of men in the community and of men to the larger world of animals and gods around them. Participation in sacrifice binds the worshiper to his community, organizes his place in that community, and implicitly obtains his consent to the violence upon which this organization is in part predi-cated. Through ritual a kind of equilibrium or justice is reached between man and his larger environment.[16]

A necessary qualification to the presentation in tragedies of specifi-cally human sacrifice is also noted by Foley:

> Human sacrifice in tragedy, however, perverts actual sacri-ficial practice, which normally prohibits the slaughter of men, and thus logically becomes a part of the social disrup-tion and crisis typical of the tragic plot.[17]

Zeitlin, in her work on the *Oresteia*, has pointed to ways in which the motif of sacrifice is recurrently adduced in that trilogy by characters who self-delusively assume the beneficial effects of sacrifice for acts whose violence is actually corrupted by impure motives and is thus not a true analogue to a properly performed, societally condoned ritual.[18] It is just such a point that will be made here about Euripides' Medea. The corruption of Medea's act and the perverseness of her appeal to a sacrificial context will be illustrated by comparison to the sacrifice of Iphigenia as to a norm invoked and in turn degenerated by Euripides. Such a contrast should not be taken to imply that the sacrifice of Iphigenia in the *Agamemnon* is not an extremely ambivalent act morally, nor that the signs of social disruption identified by Zeitlin in the world of the play are not real and significant to its themes. As the outstanding mythic and tragic *exemplum* of a parent's sacrifice of a child, however, the sacrifice of Iphigenia became accepted (if not acceptable) as a kind of standard in itself; in his evocation of and reference to that standard, Euripides chose in the *Medea* to portray a protagonist whose disruptions of proper social order were intensely more extreme and, concomitantly, less justifiable than Agamemnon's had been in the "normal" form of the motif, and so to present his audience with a dramatic world whose turmoil outreaches that of Aeschylus's House of Atreus.[19]

The initial allusion to Aeschylus is born of likeness: the drawing of the comparison points to a broad similarity of motif between the two cases—that after anguished internal debate a parent will here undertake the sacrifice of a loved child, despite the personal pain to be derived from that loss. But, as with so many of Euripides' seemingly straightforward analogies or allusions, the case for similarity rapidly unravels, as its very assertion brings leaping to mind the manifold dissimilarities between the two referents.[20]

Agamemnon's sacrifice of Iphigenia had been decreed by the will of Artemis, publicly declared by the prophet Calchas, and set upon the father with the oppressive force of *anangkē* (see, e.g., *Ag.* 218); Medea's—despite the trappings of necessity with which she imbues it (e.g., at line 1240 [discussed above, page 58])—is voluntary, freely conceived by her as the most fitting vehicle for revenge against her husband. The father's sacrifice of his daughter is necessitated when his two appointed roles as patriarch and as king/general are brought into ruinous conflict: his agonizing decision to accede to Calchas's injunction may thus be viewed as a clash either between two "rights" (his respective desires to preserve his family and to further his army's cause) or between two "wrongs" (betrayal of family as opposed to dereliction of civic duty). Medea's sacrifice of her sons, on the other hand, entails abandonment of her appointed role as mother and will bring intense personal suffering on herself; it is not counterbalanced by any opposed civic gain. In fact, as will be demonstrated in detail in chapter 6, Medea's actions are purposefully portrayed as equally ruinous in the civic realm as in the familial. Thus, when she wheels in the wavering scene from maternal anguish to heroic resolve to act, she is not, like Agamemnon, torn between two equally valid but conflicting societal directives; rather, she turns from her instinctive and societally appointed female role to perverse assumption of a masculine heroic code, obedient only to a generalized directive to seek revenge. While such a search for vengeance was an acceptable enough end in itself in the heroic world, it loses legitimacy when it requires abnegation of both the basic familial value of *philia* and proper civic allegiance. It is, further, an end which Euripides, among others, would label questionable in the fifth century, and which his Medea herself concedes, in an introspective moment, to be misdirected: "Indeed I know what ills I am about to do, but rage is winner over my deliberations—rage, which brings the greatest ills to men" (1078–80; the Greek is cited on page 59). In other words, Medea's internal debate is not between which of two right courses to undertake, or which of two wrongs to endure, but between a right and a wrong, with the wrong winning out in the end.

Finally, the reversal of the roles played by the two sexes in the compared sacrifices must not be underplayed. For a father to sacrifice a daughter: not only was such an undertaking legitimized and mitigated by Agamemnon's service (in his civic role) as preserver of general state interest over parochial family interest, but in his role as familial patriarch the father had authority over his children, who were viewed essentially as his property; troubled as the choice to sacrifice Iphigenia might be for Agamemnon, it was his choice to make. Concomitantly, female children were always a less valued commodity than their male counterparts in Greek culture; as a more marginal member of society, the female adolescent was a suitable target for the motif of virgin sacrifice, which held a fascination for Euripides.[21] The case becomes very different, however, when the sexes are reversed, and a mother is made to sacrifice her male children. First of all, as a mother who will voluntarily kill her children, Medea belies the basic stereotype of the mother who becomes fierce only in protectiveness toward her young (see ch. 2, n. 5); she is the diametric opposite of the ferocious protectress of a child against a would-be male sacrificer, a type exemplified clearly by Clytemnestra (especially as portrayed fighting the proposed sacrifice in Euripides' own *Iphigenia Aulidensis*) or by the title character of his *Hecuba*, who meets Odysseus's threat against Polyxena with the words, "I must altogether die with my daughter . . . I shall cling to her like ivy to an oak" (*Hec.* 396–98; the Greek is cited in ch. 5, n. 6). But even beyond this betrayal of her "normal" maternal role, Medea compounds her misappropriation of the masculine heroic code by usurping from her children's father his appropriately male prerogative to dispose their future—a prerogative Jason blithely but misguidedly assumes still to be his in fact as well as principle in his speech at lines 914–21.

All these anomalies rush in upon the original suggestion of similarity between Medea as sacrificer of her sons and Agamemnon as sacrificer of his daughter, crowding it out and underlining instead the abnormality of Medea's responses and actions and the inappropriateness of the metaphor of sacrifice as applied to them. Page, probably at least partially impelled to his conclusion by the unpersuasiveness of Medea's case, infers, as mentioned above, that Medea's adduction of the motif of sacrifice was not intended by the character as a disclaimer of personal responsibility for the killing she would shortly undertake. However, as an instance of argumentation by implied *exemplum* ("In sacrificing my children I join the ranks of others who have done so"), the metaphor must be aimed, nominally at least, at mitigation of the criminality of the violent deed, and at concurrent implication that it will serve a societally beneficial purpose. Ironically, this offered mitigation is immediately undercut by the numerous significant failures of parallelism which suggest themselves, and, much as the Chorus's later evocation of the parallel to Ino actually undermines the point it seems to be making, so this assumption of a sacrificial context serves to deny to Medea's victimization of her children any of the legitimacy of purpose or beneficial effect which conventionally might attach to the institution of the virgin sacrifice exemplified by Iphigenia.

IV

The *Medea*'s harsh effect on the audience is further intensified by the fact that the reactions demanded from them at various points in the play are so turbulently contradictory. Euripides did not simply *show* his audience complexities; he made them *feel* them, in the confused tumble of their own emotional responses to the characters and their actions. This is a keynote of the art of anomaly. Medea's assertion of her communality with other women inspires sympathy but eventually convicts her of the hypocrisy of a demon parading as a human being; similarly, her indecision whether she can carry through her plan makes her simultaneously more sympathetic and more horrible. The emphasis laid on her being a foreigner makes her suspect but at the same time rouses pity for her as a stranger in a strange land (see especially lines 434–35); its mitigation of the inhumane quality of her actions is belied by the strong implication that the same unnatural behavior may occur in civilized Greek women as well. The patent sophistry of Jason's feeble self-justification (see especially his "revolting" arguments, as Conacher styles them, at 526ff.)[22] is assuredly a lesser crime than Medea's shameless manipulation of Creon and Aegeus (and of Jason at 869ff.); yet somehow, paradoxically, her outright duplicity seems a part of her strength, while Jason's lesser dishonesty argues an innate weakness to his character. Yet Medea too is self-delusive (see especially 1051–52 and 1238–39). Finally, the moving and sympathetic insight into the plight of the Athenian housewife at 230ff. is counterbalanced by the adoption and repetition of standard misogynistic tags in the tradition of Hesiod and Semonides (263–66, 407–9), and the Chorus's hopeful prediction that women now will earn fair repute is proved utterly false in the end by Medea's perversion of the values that women traditionally stand for.

Formally, a similar turbulence pertains. A play originally cast in the mold of a revenge plot teeters at the end, as attention and sympathy are unexpectedly and inappropriately fastened onto the victim, on the brink of being metamorphosed into a play concerning Jason's *pathē*; this shift maximizes the confusion of sympathies and the moral tumult which the play's outcome inflicts upon its audience. A play which at its outset seems self-consciously to locate itself within a continuing tragic discourse in which a female champion of the family clashes with a male proponent of primary civic allegiance ends by denying that the conflict between men and women has any significance beyond the quibbling nastiness portrayed in its final scene and by indicting both sexes for the same ruthless egoism. Finally, the assumption of a sacrificial context for the slaying of Medea's children seeks to align her act with the sacrifice of Iphigenia as a mythic and tragic counterpart and so to mitigate its ruthlessness by implied assertion that it will be committed under a parallel yoke of necessity and to a parallel beneficial purpose; but the assertion subverts itself through its own speciousness and ends by emphasizing rather than minimizing Medea's guilt.

5

Familial *Trophē*

Medea's murder of her children was by no means her first crime against the family. Indeed, her mythic biography can read like a relentless campaign to violate the parent-child bond, and there is evidence in Euripides' play to substantiate a hypothesis that it is just so that he chose to read the Medea-saga.

Beyond the ties of affection normally presumed between parent and child, the family as an institution was capable of perpetuating itself in classical Greece because of the reciprocal nature of the duties it enjoined upon its members. The parent was expected to nurture (*trephein*) the child during the latter's period of helplessness, on the understanding that, at such a point as the parent was himself again reduced to *aporia* by the onslaught of senility, the child would take over familial responsibility and would in turn provide nurture (*trophē*) for the parent in his old age.[1] The cornerstone from which this fundamental societal construct was erected was the parent's natural love for his or her offspring and concomitant automatic assumption of a nurturing role toward that offspring; such parental response was seen as innate to the race—as, in effect, a *sine qua non* of orderly human behavior. Onto this base was added the prescript that, by having received life and nurture from the parent, the child had involuntarily (but necessarily) incurred a debt which he or she was obligated to pay back in the parent's time of need; through this metaphor of indebtedness the somewhat more artificial obligation of the child to reciprocate nurture was ratified; the Greeks thus closed the loop of reciprocity by assuring through the added weight of this ratification that the less instinctive half of the reciprocal relationship would not be slighted. The purposes of the construct were both primary and vital: through it, Greek society dealt with the complicated issues of the orderly functioning of the family, the perpetuation of the family line, the relations between the generations, and societal continuity from one generation to the next.

Both the process and the reasoning behind this system of reciprocal care are summed up succinctly by Theseus in Euripides' *Supplices* as he accedes to requests made by his mother, Aethra:

> . . . τοῖς τεκοῦσι γὰρ
> δύστηνος ὅστις μὴ ἀντιδουλεύει τέκνων—
> κάλλιστον ἔρανον· δοὺς γὰρ ἀντιλάζυται
> παίδων παρ' αὐτοῦ τοιάδ' ἂν τοκεῦσι δῷ.

> For wretched indeed is that child who fails to serve his parents in their turn—the loveliest of loans, for having given he receives in turn from his own children the same payment as he has made to his parents.

> (*Supp.* 361–64)

This concept that a reciprocity of familial *trophē* was fundamental to the order of society was one with which Euripides (along with the other tragedians) shows some preoccupation, one which he invokes recurrently in a variety of plays.[2] It is, in fact, precisely in terms of this aspect of the sacred parent-child bond that Euripides compels us to view Medea's crimes.

Medea's initial crime is to help a lover to defraud her father; in so doing, she plays the role—common in folktale—of the "ogre's daughter." Such a deceit against a parent obviously loses what legitimacy it originally had, however, if the parent is "devalued" (as Aeetes is) from ogre to normal parent and legitimate king. Medea's defection from her father, moreover, is rendered particularly radical by her parting murder of her young brother, Apsyrtus. Even the elliptical references to this murder in Euripides' play (see especially κτανοῦσα γὰρ δὴ σὸν κάσιν παρέστιον / τὸ καλλίπρωρον εἰσέβης Ἀργοῦς σκάφος: "Fresh from killing your own brother at your hearthside, you embarked on my beautiful ship, the Argo" [1334–35]; cp. 166–67) make it clear that Euripides has chosen to follow here the mythic tradition which implicates Medea with maximal guilt. A divergent tradition assigns the murder to Jason and mitigates its criminality by portraying Apsyrtus as an adult, murdered as he himself led the pursuit of Medea and the stolen fleece. Euripides' lines, on the other hand, explicitly impute the act itself to Medea and, by setting it at the sacred center of her home in Colchis (*parestion:* "at the hearth") prior to Medea's flight, indict Medea for an early familial child-murder and so escalate her guilt a step beyond that which would have attached to her for collusion in a self-defensive assault on an adult sibling.[3] Thus she neatly rounds off her crimes against her father by not only robbing him of his material wealth and herself deserting him, but—through the murder of his remaining child—by rendering him *apais* and so depriving him of any future source of *trophē*. Thus she has, in sum, betrayed his house (*oikos* or *domos*) to ruin (see especially ἀποιμώξῃ . . . οἴκους . . . οὓς προδοῦσ᾽ ἀφίκετο . . . : "she bemoans the house she betrayed to come here" [31–32]; αὐτὴ δὲ πατέρα καὶ δόμους προδοῦσ᾽ ἐμούς: "myself betraying my father and my house" [483]; cp. 502–3). This is, we shall see, only the first kingly house she will assault.

Her next step is Iolcus, Jason's native land, currently ruled by his uncle, the usurper Pelias. When Pelias declines to step down in favor of Jason even after Jason has brought home the Golden Fleece, Medea determines to eliminate Pelias. But she does not sully her own hands this time; instead she cunningly brings about the death of the father at the hands of his own daughters, who (yielding to an excess of filial piety) are persuaded to subject their father to a rejuvenation process which Medea ensures will not in fact succeed. Thus, Medea deviously turns their pious desire to spare their father the pains of senility (a desire which might be seen as the height of child-parent *trophē*) to the agency of his death. That Euripides views this second murder too as an assault by Medea on the parent-child tie is underlined by the words she herself uses to describe the crime:

Πελίαν τ᾽ ἀπέκτειν᾽, ὥσπερ ἄλγιστον θανεῖν,
παίδων ὑπ᾽ αὐτοῦ, πάντα τ᾽ ἐξεῖλον δόμον.

I killed Pelias through his children's agency—the worst way to die—and annihilated his house.

(486–87)

So falls a second kingly family and a second house (*domon:* 487) to Medea's reckless and lawless pursuit of her own and Jason's advantage. Medea herself, in indignant dialogue with Jason, later underscores her destruction of these two houses a second time:

νῦν ποῖ τράπωμαι; πότερα πρὸς πατρὸς δόμους,
οὓς σοὶ προδοῦσα καὶ πάτραν ἀφικόμην;
ἢ πρὸς ταλαίνας Πελιάδας; καλῶς γ᾽ ἂν οὖν
δέξαιντό μ᾽ οἴκοις ὧν πατέρα κατέκτανον.

Where now may I turn? To my father's house (*domous*), which I betrayed for your sake, along with my country, to come here? Or to Pelias's wretched daughters?—A fine reception they would give me in their house (*oikois*), after I killed their father.

(502–5)

In the use of both words *oikos* and *domos*, she echoes the terms in which her destruction of her father's house has previously been described (31–32, 483) and sounds notes which will prove a meaningful leitmotif as Euripides' story progresses.

These first two crimes by Medea are only briefly and allusively described by Euripides, being outside the compass of his play's action. Her third crime, however—the murder of the princess and Creon—is an essential part of this play, and in its composition Euripides takes care to signal that this episode too must be seen as a violation by Medea of the natural bond between parent and child.[4] Right from the time of Creon's entrance onto the stage, he makes it abundantly clear that his actions against Medea are prompted by his fatherly fear for his child (see, e.g., lines 283, 327, 329). Medea sizes him up quickly and rightly concludes that his love for his daughter makes him vulnerable. She proceeds to ply this vulnerability by directing her appeal for a day's grace to him *as a fellow parent:* she supplicates him by his knees and τῆς . . . νεογάμου κόρης: "your newly wedded girl" (324) and calls upon his empathy at her own children's helpless plight: οἴκτιρε δ᾽ αὐτούς· καὶ σύ τοι παίδων πατὴρ / πέφυκας: "Pity them—you too are the father of children" (344–45). Against his better judgment, Creon accedes; children are his soft spot.

Later, as Medea finally begins to reveal to the Chorus the precise form her revenge will take, her words again subtly enforce the thematic importance of the father-child relationship between Creon and the princess:

παῖδας δὲ μεῖναι τοὺς ἐμοὺς αἰτήσομαι,
οὐχ ὡς λιποῦσ' ἂν πολεμίας ἐπὶ χθονὸς
ἐχθροῖσι παῖδας τοὺς ἐμοὺς καθυβρίσαι,
ἀλλ' ὡς δόλοισι παῖδα βασιλέως κτάνω.

I shall beg that my children may stay—not as if I would leave my children here in a hostile land for my enemies to mock—but so I may by trickery kill the child of the king.

(780–83)

Medea's children are to be the tools by which she attacks the child of the king. The anaphora of *paidas / paidas*, climaxing with a change of referent in a third repetition of the word *pais* (*paida basileōs*), not only lends punch to this formulation but serves to keep the child-parent relationship at the fore of the audience's minds, underscoring in advance the fact that it is as the princess's father that Creon is to be made to suffer.[5]

The sincerity of Creon's paternal affections is set in relief by the scene (reported by the messenger) which immediately precedes the princess's death and which serves to point up, by contrast, Medea's calculating manipulation of her own children. The messenger's speech opens with an elaborate periphrasis for Medea's sons, which highlights the relationship between mother and children: τέκνων σῶν . . . δίπτυχος γονὴ: "twofold fruit of your children" (1136). This periphrasis leads into description of Jason's servants' joy at their supposition upon seeing the children that Medea and Jason have made up their quarrel; in their happiness they kiss the children's hands and blond heads (1141–42). The evocation of these vivid details both adds pathos and irony to the scene and starkly emphasizes the mother's callous willingness to victimize her own children. This egregiously unmaternal attitude is cuttingly underlined by the messenger's pointed reminder to Medea at line 1188 that the lethal garments had been brought by her children: πέπλοι δὲ λεπτοί, σῶν τέκνων δωρήματα: "the fine robes, gifts of your children."

By comparison, the motif of the tenderness of Creon's paternal feelings is picked up and elaborated, to poignant and even ghastly effect, as the messenger goes on to retail the double death of daughter and father. When the princess finally falls to the floor, succumbing to the incineration effected by her crown and her robe, her appearance is summed up in the dry phrase, πλὴν τῷ τεκόντι κάρτα δυσμαθὴς ἰδεῖν: "exceedingly hard for anyone except a parent to recognize" (1196). When Creon sees her (the emphatic first word of the report of his entrance is *patēr*: "father"), he falls on her body, groaning and embracing and kissing it, and laments:

> . . . ᾿ Ω δύστηνε παῖ,
> τίς σ᾿ ὧδ᾿ ἀτίμως δαιμόνων ἀπώλεσε;
> τίς τὸν γέροντα τύμβον ὀρφανὸν σέθεν
> τίθησιν; οἴμοι, συνθάνοιμί σοι, τέκνον.

> O wretched child, what chance has so ignominously destroyed you and makes an aged sepulcher of me, now that I'm bereaved of you? Alas, let me die along with you, my child!

> (1207–10)

The extremity of the father's grief is apparent; without his child, he would prefer not to live. Furthermore, the particular phrasing of line 1209 is again suggestive of the theme of *trophē*: an old man bereft of his child (who in turn represents his future support) is himself on the edge of the grave (*ton geronta tumbon*: "an aged sepulcher" = *tumbogeronta*: "old man on the edge of the grave" [*LSJ*]).

As the messenger speech continues after Creon's lament for his dead daughter, its macabre effect is escalated even one step more. The father's piteous plea to die along with his daughter is followed immediately by his attempt to rise again: ἐπεὶ δὲ θρήνων καὶ γόων ἐπαύσατο, / χρῄζων γεραιὸν ἐξαναστῆσαι δέμας . . . : "but when he had finished his dirges and laments and desired to raise his aged body up . . ." (1211–12). With a wry twist that borders on black comedy, the father's wish for death is revealed as a standard elegiac topic, not literally meant. However, with grim irony, it will be literally granted, for the daughter's corpse becomes the appalling agent of her father's death. As the old man attempts to rise, his flesh sticks to the incendiary robe, ὥστε κισσὸς ἔρνεσιν δάφνης: "like ivy to the shoots of laurel" (1213). The fact that *ernos*: "shoot" is frequently used metaphorically for *pais*: "child" keeps the parent-child motif in our minds, highlighting the perversion here of another standard metaphorical trope: whereas ivy is regularly viewed as clinging to a tree out of love (as of lover for lover or, as here, of parent for child), the tie that binds Creon

(= *kissos:* "ivy") to his daughter (= *ernesin:* "shoots") is the one which spells his doom.[6]

But Euripides is not yet finished with ironic inversions. The reciprocal love which binds parent to child and which originally impels Creon to embrace his daughter's corpse is metamorphosed into an adversarial force in the succeeding image, which portrays Creon's pitiful attempts to disengage himself from his daughter's clinging corpse as a wrestling match (δεινὰ . . . παλαίσματα: "dreadful wrestling match" [1214]):

ὃ μὲν γὰρ ἤθελ᾽ ἐξαναστῆσαι γόνυ,
ἣ δ᾽ ἀντελάζυτ᾽.

For he, on the one hand, was trying to lift his knee up, but she, on the other, kept hold of him.

(1215–16)

Within these one and a half lines, two subtleties are worthy of note. First, the sharp opposition of the *men . . . de:* "on the one hand . . . on the other" construction succinctly reflects the change in this particular parent-child relationship from reciprocity to antagonism. This effect is seconded by the appearance of the feminine pronoun ἥ: "she" in the *de*-clause: in an ever so understated way, this pronoun serves to reanimate the princess's corpse and to suggest that it is the daughter herself—not the robe, and not even just the thing she has become in death—who struggles here to destroy her father.

A third point of diction in these lines is also significant: that is, the choice of the verb *antelazuto.* The characteristically Euripidean poeticism *antilazomai* (*LSJ:* "take hold of or by"; "take a share of"; "receive in turn") may perhaps have been capable of suggesting the broader range of connotation of its less poetic counterpart, *antilambanomai;* if so, the meaning of the former may here be colored by the applicability of the latter to the "taking hold" of plants or the "uniting" of scions (see *LSJ* II.6). It would thus neatly pick up on the earlier image of the two bodies sticking together like ivy to a tree. More important, the word *antilazomai* in its own right seems to have had an unspecific but nonetheless strong connection in Euripides' mind with the concept of the necessity for the child to honor his parent by the return of *trophē.* All five appearances of this verb in Euripides' extant plays (see *Th. Gr. L.,* s.v.; it also appears at *Hypsipyle* fr.22.11) are in contexts in which the reciprocity of family obligations is either openly or indirectly under discussion. Thus, in the passage from the *Supplices* in which Theseus proclaims the sanctity of *trophē* (quoted above, p. 82), the verb is used to describe the justice to be meted out to the child: he will meet (*antilazutai*) in his own children the same treatment he awarded his parents. In the *Iphigenia Aulidensis*, Iphigenia grasps (*antilazumai* [1227]) Agamemnon's beard in supplication—the same beard she used to play with as she sat in his lap as a child—and speaks these words on her dashed hopes for a happy continuation of a proper father-daughter relationship:

λόγος δ' ὁ μὲν σὸς ἦν ὅδ'· ᾿Αρά σ', ὦ τέκνον,
εὐδαίμον' ἀνδρὸς ἐν δόμοισιν ὄψομαι,
ζῶσάν τε καὶ θάλλουσαν ἀξίως ἐμοῦ;
οὑμὸς δ' ὅδ' ἦν αὖ περὶ σὸν ἐξαρτωμένης
γένειον, οὗ νῦν ἀντιλάζυμαι χερί·
Τί δ' ἆρ' ἐγὼ σέ; πρέσβυν ἆρ' ἐσδέξομαι
ἐμῶν φίλαισιν ὑποδοχαῖς δόμων, πάτερ,
πόνων τιθηνοὺς ἀποδιδοῦσά σοι τροφάς;

This is what you used to say: "Will I, then, see you happy, my child, in a husband's house, living and thriving worthily of me?" And then I would reply, twining my hand around your beard, which now I grasp, "And what about you? When you are old, father, shall I admit you to the dear hospitality of my home and so pay you back nurture for nurture?"

(*IA* 1223–30)

The appearance of the same verb earlier in the play (1109) is not directly connected with *trophē,* but comes tantalizingly close, since it follows soon after Clytemnestra vents her anger at Agamemnon's proposed ἐπὶ τοῖς αὐτοῦ τέκνοις / ἀνόσια: "impieties toward his own children" (1104–5). In the *Orestes,* the verb appears twice, the first time in Orestes' admonition to Menelaus that a reciprocity of *charis* (as a parallel of *trophē*) should obtain between brothers or between brother and brother's children, just as it does between parent and child (ἀλλ' ἀντιλάζου καὶ πόνων ἐν τῷ μέρει, / χάριτας πατρῴας ἐκτίνων ἐς οὕς σε δεῖ: "Take a share as well of troubles, in their turn, and extend a father's kindnesses to those you should" [452–53]); its second appearance is in a partial repetition of these lines at 753. In each of these three passages, the verb itself is used in a different sense (to "receive in return"; to "take hold of" [the beard]; to "take a hold of / share in" [evils]), but the contexts are so strikingly similar as to justify an inference that the word was strongly connected by Euripides with the idea of reciprocity so central to the concept of familial *trophē*.

In sum, then, Medea's chosen means of wreaking vengeance on Creon has brought about another situation in which Medea attacks an enemy through his child, again demonstrating her own contempt for the normal parent-child bond, exemplified here by Creon's proper solicitude for and love of his daughter. The princess, in her turn, is an unwitting patricide (like Pelias's daughters); but, like Pelias, Creon dies ὥσπερ ἄλγιστον θανεῖν: "the worst way to die," by his daughter's agency, and, like both Aeetes and Pelias, his house is defiled.[7] The messenger speech closes with a final emphatic reference to the relation of Creon and Creusa—κεῖνται δὲ νεκροὶ παῖς τε καὶ γέρων πατὴρ / πέλας . . . : "they lie close together, the two dead bodies, child and aged father" (1220–21)—reinforcing the thematic centrality to this scene (as to the play) of familial *trophē* and its inverse, the violation of the parent-child tie.

Medea's next crime was the murder of her children. Obviously, no elaboration is needed to present this act as her most egregious violation of the tie between parent and child. However, it is notable that Medea herself twice pointedly portrays this act in terms of a future deprivation of the *trophē* to be returned by children to their elders. The first occasion is during her lament on the expected joys to be lost to her upon her children's death. A statement that the *trophē* she has expended on her children, like her labor pains, has been in vain (ἄλλως ἄρ' ὑμᾶς . . . ἐξεθρεψάμην [from *ek-trephō*: "in vain then have I reared you from childhood" [1029]; cp. the Chorus's words at 1261) is followed by an explanation of the reason she makes such a statement: that is, that they will not be there to return the favor when she is old:

ἦ μήν ποθ' ἡ δύστηνος εἶχον ἐλπίδας
πολλὰς ἐν ὑμῖν, γηροβοσκήσειν τ' ἐμὲ
καὶ κατθανοῦσαν χερσὶν εὖ περιστελεῖν,
ζηλωτὸν ἀνθρώποισι.

Once, indeed, I rested great hopes in you (wretch that I was), that you would tend me in my old age and when I

died lay out my body carefully with your own hands—an
enviable lot among men.[8]

(1032–35)

This deprivation of *trophē* will, of course, extend to Jason as well; that
is one of its major purposes. Medea makes this point evident in a later
passage. After Jason discovers that Medea has murdered their children, he unknowingly echoes Medea's words at line 1029 by lament-
ing that he has lost the children οὓς ἔφυσα κἀξεθρεψάμην: "whom I
begot and reared from childhood" (1349). Just as that earlier reference
to parent-child *trophē* led Medea into a lament for the loss of child-
parent reciprocation (*gēroboskēsein*), this second appearance of the
word *exethrepsamēn* is followed soon thereafter by a reference (though
a more indirect one) to the deprivation of the return owed by the child
to the parent, when, to one of Jason's expressions of grief over his
sons' loss, Medea makes the chilling response:

οὔπω θρηνεῖς· μένε καὶ γῆρας.

You do not yet grieve. Wait till your old age.

(1396)

With the extirpation of Jason's children and the wife by whom he
expected to have more, Medea has destroyed his house, that fine
Greek house (*oikos*) to which he boasts of having brought her from
Colchis (1330–31). Thus has she brought to fulfillment her prayer
early in the play that the whole house (*domos*) might fall (114) and
provided final validation of the Nurse's figurative assessment in the
prologue that her house (*domoi*) has already passed out of existence
(139). Thus has she fulfilled the threat leveled at Jason in line 608:

καὶ σοῖς ἀραία γ' οὖσα τυγχάνω δόμοις.

And I am a curse upon your house.

Retrospectively, Jason might appreciate a Delphic ambiguity in that
threat: whereas he would originally have heard *sois domois*: "your
house" as referring to the new house established by his marriage to
the princess, Medea's double assault has removed not only the new
house but all vestiges of the one previously established by his wedlock with her. If at the beginning of the play Jason could be justly

viewed as neglectful of his familial responsibilities and inimical to his own home (κοὐκ ἔστ᾿ ἐκεῖνος τοῖσδε δώμασιν φίλος: "And he is no friend to this house (*dōmasin*)" [77]), in the end she who lamented his carelessness has been proven its arch-foe.

The crimes of the mythographical Medea do not end coincidentally with the end of Euripides' play; they continue after she takes up residence with Aegeus in Athens. That Euripides intended the audience of his present play to think forward to this later phase in the Medea-saga is clearly indicated first by the very inclusion of the Aegeus-episode and then by the peculiar emphases laid by its dramatic cast.[9]

Later in the Medea-saga, Aegeus, with whom Medea has formed a sexual alliance, is made to feel insecure in the kingship of Athens by the arrival in town of a much-touted monster-killing stranger, clearly a mighty hero. Unbeknownst to Aegeus, this stranger is his son, sired in foreign parts in incomprehension of the Delphic Oracle's metaphorical stricture not to "loose the jutting foot of the wineskin" until he arrived home in Athens. Medea, on the other hand, knowing full well the stranger's identity, stirs Aegeus up to the murder of his unrecognized son; it is only by the fortuitous, nick-of-time recognition of birth tokens that Theseus is spared death by poison at his own father's instigation. When the *anagnōrisis* takes place, Medea is once again banished.[10]

The ironies of the situation are evident. The audience who view the Aegeus-episode of Euripides' *Medea* must be aware that the Medea of myth will later make an even further attack against the parent-child tie by instigating the poisoning of Theseus by his father. This foreknowledge would clearly color their appreciation of the scene in the present play in which Medea promises that, in return for the promise of sanctuary from Aegeus, she will provide him with the "fruit of children" (παίδων γονάς [717]). The gap between the predictions made by Medea and the outcome of the action as foreknown by the audience creates a distinct irony. First, at least in the sense expected by Aegeus, Medea will not make good her promise, for Aegeus will proceed directly from his meeting with her to the home of Pittheus (so he tells us at lines 683ff.), where he will sire Theseus on the daughter of this so-called "dearest of spear-friends." Further, if one follows the mythic tradition in which Theseus is destined to be Aegeus's only-begotten son, Medea will at a later date do her best to *return* Aegeus to *apaidia*.

If one thinks forward instead to the variant tradition by which, at a later date, Aegeus and Medea together have a son, Medus, then in fact Medea *does* provide Aegeus with the "fruit of children"—but by a means far different from the potions that she now promises him. The sexual overtone of the language Medea uses at line 1385 to describe to Jason her own future plans (Αἰγεῖ συνοικήσουσα τῷ Πανδίονος: "to live with Pandion's son, Aegeus"; for the sexual connotation of *sunoikeō*, cp. line 242) slyly hints at this outcome.

Aegeus relates the oracle's riddling response to Medea specifically because he hopes her superior intellect will provide him some immediate insight into its meaning. She conceals any understanding she may have, thus sending Aegeus off to the clutches of the equally unscrupulous Pittheus. Instead she responds with promises which may be construed either as falsehoods (if Theseus is to be Aegeus's only child) or as Delphic ambiguities (if she will herself bear him a son). One can scarcely hear Medea's boast to Aegeus at line 716—εὕρημα δ' οὐκ οἶσθ' οἷον ηὕρηκας τόδε: "you know not what luck you have come upon here"—without considering how true it is, but in a startlingly different sense from that meant to be intelligible to Aegeus. He will, one fears, come to rue the day when Medea succeeds in arriving at his house (ἐάνπερ εἰς ἐμοὺς ἔλθῃς δόμους: "if you get to my house" [727]—just as all the other kings whose houses she affects have regretted or will regret her presence and effect on their homes.

Of course, the total extent of the irony of this passage—that Medea promises παίδων γονάς: "fruits of children" to Aegeus while planning, or beginning to plan, the extirpation of her own offspring, that she will reduce Jason to just the same state of *apaidia* she here promises to cure Aegeus of (but will later try to inflict on him again)—will only be revealed to the audience retrospectively as the action of the play proceeds. But even considering the limited knowledge of future events vouchsafed to the audience at this point in the plot, one can hardly help feeling that Medea's duping of an unknowing Aegeus begins far in advance of her concealment from him of the grown Theseus's identity.

Thus, Medea's crimes, both inside and outside the play, may be seen as resolute attacks on the natural ties between parent and child and on the family as an institution which allows for societal continuity. If before Euripides' play the Medea of myth did not actually murder her own children, that was practically her only omission in the depredation of this sacred familial relationship. By adding that element to her biography, Euripides has essentially brought her story, as he chooses to read it, to its logical climax. A particular mode of his expression of these attacks is recurrently to emphasize one aspect of the parent-child bond: the obligatory reciprocity of nurture by which the family perpetuates itself. Through acts of violence which are directly disruptive of reciprocal familial *trophē*, Medea's repeated stamping out of *oikoi* sets her in opposition to the traditional role of the woman as protectress of the household and champion of the family. Jason has negated *her* house by taking a new wife (τῶν τε λέκτρων / ἄλλα βασίλεια κρείσσων / δόμοισιν ἐπέστα: "another queen commands your house (*domoisin*), mistress of your bed," says the Chorus to Medea (443–45); Medea later echoes them: γυναῖκ' ἐφ' ἡμῖν δεσπότιν δόμων ἔχει: "he has a woman as mistress of his house (*domōn*) in place of me" (694). Once this situation has come to pass, Medea's response is to renounce with the utmost finality her wifely role as a vehicle for the continuation of the male line. She does so by reducing Jason to *apaidia* and adding his house to the roster of those kingly houses that tradition has her assail. Euripides thus not only reverses with biting irony the expectation aroused at the beginning of the play that she will stand for female primary allegiance to the family; he also incarnates her as the lethal enemy of the social order the Athenians had carefully constructed from the dual tenets of a proper complementary balance between the sexes and of a reciprocal obligation of care between the generations.

6

Civic *Trophē*

The theme of *trophē* in the *Medea* is not limited to the author's treatment of the parent-child tie. The family and the larger societal group represented by the state were two concepts which, in ancient Greece, were both intimately associated and set in disjunction against each other. Through a complex causation born at once of the similarities and dissimilarities of the two entities, a standard metaphorical identification arose between family and state; that is, that the state is like a larger family, which plays a role of "parent" to the citizen-child.[1] Accordingly, the *polis* becomes the *mētropolis*: "mother city." Concomitantly with the generalized adoption of this metaphor comes particularized application to the state of the sacred obligation of *trophē* which bound both parent and child. In this civic form of *trophē*, the city is seen as nurturing the citizen (offering him a land to live in and extending him the protection of its laws) while the citizen is expected in return to nurture the city by pledging his loyalty and ungrudging support.

The concept of *trophē* thus becomes a quadripartite idea, subsuming the obligations of parent to child, child to parent, state to citizen, and citizen to state. The intertwining of these several elements into a central and unified tragic theme has been demonstrated by Daly for the *Oedipus Coloneus* of Sophocles.[2] The same combination of themes is at the heart of Euripides' *Medea*, written over two decades earlier—

but to an effect startlingly at odds with Sophocles' masterful encomium to Athens.

Just as Medea's crimes may be viewed as assaults on the parent-
child bond, so they reflect, in varying degrees, violation of the figurative civic aspect of *trophē* as well. The aid Medea gives Jason in his
theft of the Golden Fleece is painted as betrayal of country equally as
crime against father; in the passages in which Medea laments her
misbegotten transferral of allegiance from home to Jason (cited in ch.
3, n. 7), mention of country (whether as *gaia, patris, patra,* or *polis*)
occurs as often as mention of father; most often the two appear in
combination, as in ὦ πάτερ, ὦ πόλις: "O father, o city!" (166). Medea's
failure to repay, as citizen, the nurture she had received from the state
is given explicit expression at line 1332: πατρός τε καὶ γῆς προδότιν ἥ
σ᾽ ἐθρέψατο [from *trephō*]: "betrayer of your father and of the land
which reared you." In return, she is reciprocally bereft of the support
her city could offer her; she is (unlike the thankful Chorus) *apolis:*

> σοὶ μὲν πόλις θ᾽ ἥδ᾽ ἐστὶ καὶ πατρὸς δόμοι
> βίου τ᾽ ὄνησις καὶ φίλων συνουσία,
> ἐγὼ δ᾽ ἔρημος ἄπολις οὖσ᾽ ὑβρίζομαι
> πρὸς ἀνδρός . . .

> You have this city and your father's home, and enjoyment
> of life and the company of your friends. I, bereft and de-
> prived of a city, am mocked by my husband.

> (253–56)

Medea calls this loss to mind most acutely at the point when Creon
announces his edict of banishment from Corinth for her and her sons:

> ὦ πατρίς, ὥς σου κάρτα νῦν μνείαν ἔχω.

> O fatherland, how very mindful *now* I am of you!

> (328)

The murder of King Pelias, far from winning Jason back his proper
role as head of state in Iolcus, outrages the citizens so badly that the
couple is expelled. In Corinth Medea outrages the king's house; the
messenger's description of her actions at line 1130 (. . . τυράννων
ἑστίαν ἠκισμένη . . . : "befouling the hearth [*hestian*] of kings") will later
in the play be echoed by allusion to her previous murder of Apsyrtus

parestion: "at your hearth" (1334).³ Thus, in Corinth Medea betrays a third city much as she had betrayed her own and Jason's native lands, belying the early promise of a mutually beneficial civic relationship alluded to somewhat cryptically by the Nurse in the prologue:

οὐδ' ἂν . . .
. . . κατῴκει τήνδε γῆν Κορινθίαν
ξὺν ἀνδρὶ καὶ τέκνοισιν, ἁνδάνουσα μὲν
φυγῇ *πολιτῶν* ὧν ἀφίκετο χθόνα,
αὐτή τε πάντα ξυμφέρουσ' Ἰάσονι.

Nor would she then be dwelling in this Corinthian land with her husband and children, in her exile bringing pleasure to the citizens (*politōn*) to whose land she is come, and herself complying in everything to Jason.

(9–13)

So too her murder of her children prevents realization of Jason's ambition that his sons by Medea will join their future half-brothers to become the leaders of the city of his exile (916ff.).

As she contemplates flight from Corinth, Medea delays implementation of her revenge until she can foresee a means of securing from a new source the civic protection she has forfeited now in three cities (Colchis, Iolcus, and Corinth):

καὶ δὴ τεθνᾶσι· τίς με δέξεται *πόλις*;

And now presume them dead—what city (*polis*) will receive me?

(386)

If Medea has no respect for the sanctity of the reciprocal support of city and citizen, she does not, it seems, lose a self-interested respect for the one-sided advantages she may reap from association with yet another adoptive *mētropolis.* But even in her relations with Athens, her next port of call, she will betray the prescripts of civic *trophē:* the murder of Theseus which she will attempt at a later point in the saga could only be viewed by the Athenian audience as a heinous attempt to defraud them in advance of their greatest national hero.

Furthermore, this theme of civic *trophē* is central to the two scenes in which Medea meets with kings (Creon, then Aegeus). In these passages, I shall argue, Euripides subverts yet another set of "normal" values, nihilistically effacing one more "given" assumed by his audience.

It has often been noted that the *Medea* affords glimpses of a characteristic Athenian patriotism. The most obvious locus for such patriotic coloring in the play is the great ode (824ff.) in which the Chorus fervently and explicitly sings the praises of the playwright's and audience's mother city. This ode is commonly taken to exemplify "the patriotic exaltation with which Euripides entered the period of war."[4] The second clear locus for patriotism in the *Medea* is the appearance of Aegeus as the prototype of the stock fair-ruling and nontyrannical Athenian king, prone to offering safe refuge (at some cost to himself) to ill-beset wanderers. This tragic typology has its roots in Aeschylus and becomes more common in the war years following the production of the *Medea*.[5]

Along with notice of Euripides' exhibitions of patriotism in the play has come mention of the slander that accrued to Euripides at some point after production of the *Medea*: that Euripides had accepted a bribe from the Corinthians (who in 431 B.C. were in a state of open enmity with the Athenians) to saddle Medea instead of them with the murder of her children. Page notes that, while the substance of this *poluaikos logos* should be given no credence, its existence nonetheless suggests that one reaction to Euripides' version of the child-murder had been to explain it away by impugning his motives: "There can be no doubt that Euripides incurred grave censure for presenting a play in which a crime traditionally charged against Corinthians was transferred from them to Medea. The poet was obviously open to the charge that his play was unpatriotic. . . ."[6] Minimal critical notice, however, seems to have been taken of the paradox which results from simultaneous assertions that Euripides' play is patriotic and unpatriotic.

When Creon enters the stage at line 271, bringing news of fresh disaster (her banishment from Corinth, along with her children) to a still-sympathetic Medea, his opening words are (as Page notes, *ad loc.*) abrupt and pugnacious. He fears Medea, as he tells us at line 282, and rightly so, the audience may think, since his entrance has followed hard upon Medea's extraction of an oath of silence from the Chorus concerning her future revenge. Yet his autocratic quickness to visit further victimization on an as yet unoffending Medea and on her innocent children as well cannot be fully explained away even by the fact that his fear is reasonable. In fact, Creon's blusterings upon his entrance are suggestive of a typology familiar to the democratic Athenian audience, that of the illegitimately tyrannical king.[7] In tragedy, the early kings of Athens were typically portrayed as so fair-minded as to make the later evolution of the Athenian *polis* into a democracy seem not only logical but almost inevitable. On the other hand, kings of other cities might more frequently fit the mold of the tyrant: see, for example, the Creon of Sophocles' *Antigone* or, at a later date, the elaborate contrast in the *Oedipus Coloneus* between the Theban Creon and the Athenian Theseus. In Euripides' *Medea*, Creon's opening words plainly set him in the worse tradition and pave the way for a contrast between this Corinthian king and the Athenian Aegeus, who will appear later to offer refuge to the banished heroine. The patriotic coloring of such a contrast would have been heightened by the contemporaneous political hostility between the two cities.

However, the clarity of the antithesis as it immediately suggests itself to the audience (tyrannical [= bad] Corinthian vs. proto-democratic [= good] Athenian) is quickly clouded by the playwright. Not only will the play's eventual outcome prove that Creon's initial fear of Medea is all too justified, but even in the short run Creon will prove himself both a sympathetic character and a right-minded one, according to the Athenian definition. As the scene continues, it becomes clear that Creon's two ruling concerns are love for his daughter and love for his city. To Medea's charge that he fails to reverence her supplication sufficiently, he responds with a statement of priorities:

φιλῶ γὰρ οὐ σὲ μᾶλλον ἢ δόμους ἐμούς.

Yes, for I do not regard you more than I regard my home and family.

(327)

His sense of loyalty to his own evokes from Medea a lament for the home now lost to her (328; quoted above); Creon in turn amplifies his feelings for his homeland:

πλὴν γὰρ τέκνων ἔμοιγε φίλτατον πολύ.

Ah, the fatherland—except for my children, dearest thing to me by far.

(329)

His bipartite allegiance to family and city reflects a proper concern for both the personal and civic aspects of *trophē*: as both father and king, Creon aligns himself firmly on the side of legitimacy.

When Medea appeals to him on behalf of her children, Creon can no longer maintain his tyrannical façade; he gives in to her importunings. The speech in which he reverses his earlier resolve to drive Medea out forthwith signals a turnaround in his character as initially presented to the audience:

> ἥκιστα τοὐμὸν λῆμ᾽ ἔφυ τυραννικόν,
> αἰδούμενος δὲ πολλὰ δὴ διέφθορα·
> καὶ νῦν ὁρῶ μὲν ἐξαμαρτάνων, γύναι,
> ὅμως δὲ τεύξῃ τοῦδε.

> My will is by nature the opposite of tyrannical; rather, I have spoiled things many a time through regard for others. So, woman, while even now I see that it is a mistake, I will nonetheless give you what you ask.

> (348–51)

Even against his better judgment, he softens. Far from being harshly tyrannical, as his initial characterization projected him, he cannot maintain a tyrannical posture even when it would clearly be the wiser course to do so. His soft spot is children; his second major concern is the welfare of his city. He is, then, a picture of upright piety and humanity in his adoption of right attitudes within the societal system of *trophē*. Ironically, it is his very virtues which will cause his destruction and that of all he holds most dear.

The tyrannical Creon of Sophocles' *Antigone* softens in the end, persuaded by Tiresias that he has adopted too rigid and autocratic a stand. Tragically, his change of heart comes too late to save the lives of Antigone, Haemon, and his wife; it is never in doubt, however, that the reversal of his earlier posture was *right*. Put the same motif into the hands of the more cynical Euripides, and significant inversions are promptly made. When Euripides' Creon is tyrannical, he is right. When he yields to persuasion, he is wrong. A tyrannical stance is the only thing which might have saved him and his beloved daughter; his reversion to his more humane self destroys them both. The audience's retrospective realization of these reversals, once the plot has unfolded to reveal Medea's true intent, must undoubtedly be unsettling.

As previously discussed, the extremity of Medea's plight when she is forsaken by Jason results from the fact that a woman's normal recourse upon divorce (return to her father's protection) is precluded in her case. Her predicament is specifically that she is *apolis*, as she herself points out to the Chorus at lines 252–58. Creon's subsequent proclamation banishing her from Corinth aggravates her situation. After the intervention of Medea's scenes with Creon and Jason, the Chorus picks up the theme previously sounded by Medea, that unlike them she is bereft of any city's protection, and sounds a fervent prayer that a like fate never fasten upon them:

> ὦ πατρίς, ὦ δώματα, μὴ
>   δῆτ᾽ ἄπολις γενοίμαν
> τὸν ἀμηχανίας ἔχουσα
> δυσπέρατον αἰῶν᾽,
> οἰκτροτάτων ἀχέων.
> θανάτῳ θανάτῳ πάρος δαμείην
> ἀμέραν τάνδ᾽ ἐξανύσασα· μό-
> χθων δ᾽ οὐκ ἄλλος ὕπερθεν ἢ
> γᾶς πατρίας στέρεσθαι.

O fatherland, o home, may I never be left without a country, living that hard life of helplessness and pitiable sorrow. I would rather bow to death—yes, to death—and bring this day to an end. No hardship is worse than to lose one's native land.

(643–51)

This emotional chorus is followed immediately (and significantly) by Aegeus's entrance onto the stage at line 663. With Aegeus's arrival, the second half of the antithesis suggested by Creon's autocratic entrance supplies itself to an audience which, seconds before, has been drawn to contemplation of the blessed security attainable only in the bosom of one's homeland. This is the stuff of which patriotic coloring is made. Here is the noble-souled Athenian king, who will offer safe harbor to the shipwrecked heroine. He will relieve her of her burden by offering her a new city, the fairest one of all, the audience's native Athens. And, indeed, Aegeus lives up to expectations. After an initial period of absorption with his own problems, he graciously grants Medea release from hers.[8] The Chorus's valedictory judgment on the

Athenian king reinforces the sense that Aegeus appears here as the converse to the tyrannical king:

ἀλλά σ' ὁ Μαίας πομπαῖος ἄναξ
πελάσειε δόμοις, ὧν τ' ἐπίνοιαν
σπεύδεις κατέχων πράξειας, ἐπεὶ
γενναῖος ἀνήρ,
Αἰγεῦ, παρ' ἐμοὶ δεδόκησαι.

May the son of Maia, our escorting lord, guide you home, and may you achieve the purposes you strive so eagerly after, for you seem, in my judgment, Aegeus, a noble man.

(759–63)

Again, however, as in the meeting of Creon and Medea, a situational irony will later become apparent to the audience, for Aegeus's generous act of hospitality toward Medea will prove him a dupe and cause the pollution of his so fair city, as the Chorus explicitly informs us at lines 824–50, discussed below.

Aegeus promises refuge to Medea in expectation that she will in turn provide him with the ability to beget children (see especially line 721). Aegeus is *apais;* Medea is *apolis.* The two aspects of *trophē,* personal and civic, are central to this scene, as each character seeks to remedy his/her own lack through the joining of resources with the other one. Aegeus will follow through on his pledge, the audience knows, for received myth tells them so; Medea will not. Indications that Medea foresees this outcome and deliberately plays on Aegeus's vulnerability to achieve her own selfish end have been discussed above (pp. 000ff.). But one particular aspect of the encounter with Aegeus points up most emphatically Medea's conscious imposture in this scene and the concomitant devaluation of Aegeus's role from that of noble benefactor to that of easy mark for Medea's deceptions. Medea demands oaths of Aegeus.[9] To his somewhat indignant response (733), she explains that this is merely a precautionary measure, intended to spare Aegeus himself further stress, as well as to safeguard her own future (734–40). Her presentation convinces Aegeus (if not, perhaps, the suspicious audience member), as the congratulatory tone of his capitulation (741–45) makes clear.

At a later point in the action, once Medea has killed the Corinthian king and princess and sacrificed her own children, one may assume that Aegeus, if not bound by oaths, would have reneged on his promise to Medea, and justly so, as her actions since have been so morally repugnant as to negate any previous commitments. In swearing them, then, he is like a fish biting the hook.

Moreover, a comparison with a similar scene in the *Oedipus Coloneus* indicates that Medea's demand for oaths not only would be appreciated retrospectively as a form of deliberate deception, but even at its own point in the action would have resonated dissonantly. At *OC* 631ff., Theseus declares Oedipus a citizen of Athens, thus promising him the city's protection against those from Thebes who would forcibly return him there. As in the Aegeus-scene in the *Medea,* the question of how firm the king's promise will be under siege occurs to the parties involved. But the answer to the question differs radically from one play to the other, as this exchange between Theseus and Oedipus on the subject of oaths makes clear:

> Θη. θάρσει τὸ τοῦδέ γ' ἀνδρός· οὔ σε μὴ προδῶ.
> Οι. οὔτοι σ' ὑφ' ὅρκου γ' ὡς κακὸν πιστώσομαι.
> Θη. οὔκουν πέρα γ' ἂν οὐδὲν ἢ λόγῳ φέροις.
>
> Th. Fear not, at least not so far as *this* man is concerned: I will not betray you.
> Oed. Nor shall I secure your good faith by oaths, as if you were a base man.
> Th. If you did, you would gain no more than through my word.

(*OC* 649–51)

Did Sophocles write this passage as a deliberate corrective to the values of expediency referred to in Euripides' Aegeus-scene? Or did the later passage merely reflect a more standard version of the oath-motif (*Gentlemen do not need oaths; it is crass of you to demand them*)? It is impossible to say with any degree of certainty. It is clear, however, that Medea's demand for oaths from Aegeus is less than generous and would be perceived so. And the fact that Aegeus was thus tricked into sticking by a promise which he might otherwise justifiably have spurned is likewise significant.

Aegeus, then, as set against the blustering Creon, is immediately perceptible to his audience as a welcome contrast, an incipient Athenian democrat in a time of illegitimate tyrants. However, the outcome of the play's action will prove him a gull. Unlike Creon, his picture is painted in resoundingly positive terms. Like Creon, however, his virtues put him at Medea's mercy. The antithesis which the playwright *seems* to set up, drawing on his audience's normal expectations, is negated by the similarity in the two kings' eventual fates. Creon, when by being tyrannical he seems to be doing wrong, is doing right. Aegeus, when he adheres to the more equitable and humane policy expected of a good Athenian king, is a dupe; he would have served his city better, like Creon, if he had been a little more *turannikos*.

It may be added that we have here yet one more instance where a plausible "truth" initially presented to us by the playwright turns out to have been illusory, or true-but-untrue. Toward the beginning of the play, a righteous Medea cries out against Jason's breach of the oaths by which he had bound himself upon marriage. She will renew this charge several times as the play progresses. Medea's indignation at this betrayal has prompted Paley to characterize her as a "young and forlorn princess" victimized by a too innocent trust in a stranger's oaths.[10] Page adds, aptly, that "the contrast of truthful barbarian and lying Greek had long been a commonplace."[11] But the antithesis thus seemingly set up—female/barbarian trust in honorable behavior versus male (cp. 410ff.)/Greek deceit—is shattered at that point in the play when Medea herself, the supposed naïve, purposefully and with malice aforethought (unlike Jason) uses oaths to bind an overly trusting Aegeus (Greek male) to a self-destructive course of action. The shocking disingenuousness of this action by Medea is, of course, intensified by the implication that she herself knows all along, like the audience, that Aegeus's childlessness will end all on its own and before Medea joins him in Athens. In the final scene of the play, Medea recapitulates her earlier charges against Jason by answering his curse with the question: τίς δὲ κλύει σοῦ θεὸς ἢ δαίμων, / τοῦ ψευδόρκου καὶ ξειναπάτου: "What god, what heavenly being will heed you, who are false to your oaths and deceiving of strangers?" (1391–92). If Jason was *pseudorkos:* "false to his oath" and *xeinapatēs:* "deceiving of *xenoi* [=strangers, foreigners, or one's host or guest]" toward Medea at the start of the play's action, by all accounts Medea's treatment of and intentions toward Aegeus (her soon-to-be host) have at its end even more legitimately earned for her the same two epithets.

Along with her repeated and characteristic attack on the parent-child bond and on reciprocal parent-child nurture, then, Medea is guilty of a parallel subversion of civic *trophē*. During Medea's initial dialogue with Creon, as she tries to disarm the king's fear of her, she makes the duplicitous claim that οὐχ ὧδ᾽ ἔχει μοι—μὴ τρέσῃς ἡμᾶς, Κρέον—/ὥστ᾽ ἐς τυράννους ἄνδρας ἐξαμαρτάνειν: "You need not fear me, Creon. I am not in a position to sin against the power of kings" (307–8). Even at that point in the dramatic action, the assertion inspires little credence: her crimes against two kings (her father and Pelias) and their cities (Colchis and Iolcus) form the background of the play; these crimes have rendered not only her but also Jason *apolis*. As the play continues, she will in fact move against a third king, Creon, and will cast the royal house of Corinth into disarray by killing both the king himself and the daughter who would continue his line and provide the city with its future rulers.[12] She thus also deprives a third city and citizenry of the *trophē* they receive most signally from their king.

The cast of the Aegeus-episode plainly invites the Athenian audience to think into the mythographical future and foresee Medea's coming attempt to kill Theseus, which represents an attack on yet a fourth king, her current savior Aegeus. Thus, Medea's final act of violence against citizen-state *trophē* will be aimed at the audience's own city of Athens. This point is underlined by the highly emotional chorus which begins at line 824.

Immediately after Aegeus leaves the stage, Medea reveals to the Chorus her plan to murder her children. After this revelation, the Chorus launches into a lyrical, highly colored encomium of Athens. Through one strophe and its antistrophe, they evoke light, clarity, and sanctity as the characterizing elements of the city topographically, morally, and aesthetically. Patriotic coloring? Clearly, yes—as far as this sequence of strophe and antistrophe goes. The incongruity of the placement of this acknowledgment of Athens's supremacy into the mouths of Corinthian women, at a time when relations between the two cities had deteriorated markedly, might especially appeal to patriots in the audience. But those who would sit back and bask in this eulogy of their holy metropolis will be brought up short by the opening lines of the Chorus's second strophe (rendered here as it appears in Page's version of the text):

πῶς οὖν ἱερῶν ποταμῶν
ἢ πόλις ἢ φίλων
πόμπιμός σε χώρα
τὰν παιδολέτειραν ἕξει,
τὰν οὐχ ὁσίαν μετ᾽ ἄλλων;

> How then will a city of sacred rivers, a land that grants safe
> passage to its friends, yet sustain you, the murderess of
> your children, you the impure amid others?

(846–50)

The rude effect of this query has not been sufficiently considered by
those who speak of the first two stanzas' fervent patriotism—for any
self-congratulatory feelings of civic pride in the audience must be cut
short by the succeeding image of the pollution to be brought upon
their chaste homeland by Medea's entry into it.[13] Understated though
these lines may be, after the fulsome terms of the previous stanzas
they are sufficient to open up a series of ominous musings on the part
of the audience. Received myth would assure them that Medea had
been admitted to Athens along with her pollution. Has their fair land,
then, been contaminated by receiving her? Have its sacred rivers (see
ἱερῶν ποταμῶν at 846; cp. τοῦ καλλινάου τ' ἐπὶ Κηφισοῦ ῥοαῖς: "at the
streams of the beautifully flowing Cephisus" [835])—the primordial
nurturers to whom boys attaining manhood dedicated a symbolic
repayment for the *trophē* received from their homeland[14]—been be-
fouled by contact with Medea's diseased disrespect for *trophē* in all its
aspects? What kind of ruler is it who would, even unwittingly, bring
such pollution into his city? By his gullibility, has their beloved ancestral king admitted into the city he is charged to preserve and protect
an impurity which, once contracted, may linger on even to the present day, an impurity embodied by Medea's breaches of the sacred and
fundamental ties, both familial and civic, by which human beings
undertake to live together?

The clarity of the easy patriotism which the poet seemingly seeks to
arouse with the Chorus's glittering evocation of Athens's pristine
beauty is tainted by these haunting questions. One more revered
truth is assailed as the Athenians are reluctantly drawn to see a chink
in their pervasive assumption of virtue.

Conclusion

The reciprocal nurture required of human society is a primary thematic focus of Euripides' *Medea*. The theme is picked out repeatedly, both in the family relationships portrayed in the play and in the characters' relation to their larger society. In a view of natural order succinctly expressed by Aristotle (see p. 00 above) and unchallenged by the vast majority of Euripides' audience and even by most who have lived in the two thousand years following his play, the bond between parent and child, and especially mother and child, stands as the most fundamental and unquestionable of the *nomoi brotōn*. The full power of Euripides' *Medea* lies in his protagonist's recurrent assaults on that sacred relationship. Those of Medea's offenses which precede the dramatic time of the play are merely sketched: her earlier crimes against her own father through the theft of the fleece and murder of her brother, and her attack on Jason's uncle through the would-be filial ministrations of his daughters. The heroine's later escapade in Athens, the attempt to engineer Theseus's death at his unknowing father's hand, is merely suggested by the play's emphasis on Aegeus's lamentable childlessness and Medea's intended involvement in it. The murder of the Corinthian princess and the gruesome way in which her father's affection for her is turned to the agency of both their deaths are graphically and emphatically detailed, as is the climactic crime by which Medea deprives herself and Jason of the fruits of children and the support which those children would later represent to their old age. In each of these assaults, the particularized description of Medea's actions makes it clear that the playwright is cataloguing not only Medea's elimination of her perceived enemies, but the essential scorn for family ties which underlies her actions. Yet even "scorn" is not a strong enough word: to attack her father through murder of his son, to attack Pelias through his daughters, to attack Creon through his daughter's corpse, to attack Jason through the loss of his sons, to attack Theseus through his unknowing father—all suggest a diabolical hostility not just to the victims themselves but to the ties which bind them and all humanity to one another.

Within this broad scheme, Euripides' introduction into the myth of the mother's purposeful slaying of her own children may be appreciated as the perfect culmination of the story as he has chosen to present it. She has despoiled other parents of their children, other children of their parents. She has destroyed her own father. All that is left is for her to turn her deadly hand on her children. When she does so, the character commits the ultimate breach of the parent-child relationship, and the playwright's portrayal of the breakdown of this most basic bond becomes emblematic of the ultimate breakdown in human order. Hesiod too had envisioned the total decay of society:

> And forthwith they will dishonor their aging parents; they
> will blame them, speaking with harsh words—hardhearted,
> and with no thought of the vengeance of the gods; nor
> would they give their parents return for their nurture.
>
> (*Op.* 185–88; Greek quoted p. 27)

But the depravity of the child-murdering mother goes one step beyond the worst sin against *trophē* that Hesiod could conceive; it is, symbolically, the nadir of human depravity.[1]

Starting with the prologue of the play, the full virtuosity of Euripidean dramatic technique is turned to the task of accentuating the horror innate to the heroine's climactic crime. Throughout the first half of the play, he concentrates his dramatic skills on the creation of a heightened atmosphere of foreboding and tension, centered on the question of the children's eventual fate. He hints that Medea will harm them; he negates those hints. He pulls the audience's expectations alternately this way and that. In the second half of the play, after Medea's plan is openly revealed to the audience, he turns his artistry to intensification of dramatic tension as he leads the audience to the awful climax. Through Medea's waverings, as through earlier assertions of her ordinary womanhood, and by filtering the audience's vision of her intent through the lens of an uncomprehending Chorus, Euripides renders that climax all the more powerful.

By further assuming a metaphorical identification of familial *trophē* and civic *trophē*, Euripides makes his character an enemy not only of the family but of the state. The expectation raised early in the audience that this play will treat of the standard tragic antinomy between loyalty to family and allegiance to state (in the tradition of the *Oresteia* and the *Antigone*) fades at the realization that Medea is here presented as disruptive of *both* sets of values. Along with her varied attacks on members of her own and others' families, she serially violates the royal houses and disrupts the proper civic functioning of four cities: Colchis, Iolcus, Corinth, and Athens. Four kings, whether father, friend, or foe, are equally subjected to her ruthless pursuit of her own ends; every city which has offered her nurture is ravaged or polluted by her presence.

Euripides' Medea may be said, in sum, to be the incarnation of disorder. Social order, civic order both fall before her triumphant *anomia*. And, because the proper functioning of the dictates of *trophē* is taken by the playwright as normative of cosmic order, when she is done, there is nothing left.

A pointed comparison may be made to the Cyclops of Homer's *Odyssey*. Isolated from others, with his individual realm ringed round by other Cyclopes but not truly confederated with them, he declines to enter into any social linkages:

τοῖσιν δ᾽ οὔτ᾽ ἀγοραὶ βουληφόροι οὔτε θέμιστες,
ἀλλ᾽ οἵ γ᾽ ὑψηλῶν ὀρέων ναίουσι κάρηνα
ἐν σπέσσι γλαφυροῖσι, θεμιστεύει δὲ ἕκαστος
παίδων ἠδ᾽ ἀλόχων, οὐδ᾽ ἀλλήλων ἀλέγουσι.

These men have neither laws (*themistes*) nor assemblies for counsel; they dwell amid the peaks of lofty mountains in hollowed out caves, and each one is law over (*themisteuei*) his wives and children, and they have no care for one another.

(*Od.* 9.112–15)

In his dealings with Odysseus, Polyphemus's chief crime is to refuse to honor the laws of *xenia:* "guest-friendship," from which the Greeks had constructed a complex code of moral behavior designed to extend the protective umbrella of social order over the man who travels beyond the bounds of his own homeland. Polyphemus's only deference to this sacred societal system is his mocking promise that, as *xeinēïon:* "guest-gift," he will eat Odysseus last (9.369–70). He thus stands as an archetype of the individual who resists the impulse to socialization, who is immune from the necessary, but fragile compacts by which people undertake to live together to mutual benefit. In this immunity, he is not, it should be stressed, an outlaw; in fact, just after the blinding of Polyphemus, when his neighbors rally about, made curious by his screams, he and they are seen to be loosely connected by generalized goodwill, an inchoate urge to confederacy (9.399ff.). He is, rather, representative of a pre-*themis*, or pre-law, existence. Odysseus's demand that Polyphemus ascribe to his own societal code is, then, anachronistic, for the Cyclopes are "of" an earlier social time than Odysseus.

Euripides' characterization of Medea draws on this literary prototype as established by Homer. Medea too is a rampant individualist, ruthlessly declining to set aside one whit of self-interest to subscribe to the familial and civic codes which are the fabric of social living. Several important distinctions may be made, however, between her and her literary ancestor, distinctions which reveal not only that her lawlessness overreaches that of her predecessor but also that the effect achieved by her presentation to an audience differs both in degree and in kind from that of the Cyclops story.

Unlike Homer's Cyclops, Euripides' Medea cannot be said to be pre-*themis*. "Primitive," yes, precisely in her exemption from the prescripts of society. A foreigner and a sorceress as well, but as Euripides has written her story she has come from a land where the same expectations of respect for familial and social obligations pertained as in Greece, as all her invocations of father and homeland betrayed make clear; up to the time of Jason's defection she has, further, conformed in all respects to the Corinthian familial and civic codes (see especially lines 10–13), and as wife she is confined by Greek societal patterns as relentlessly as any ordinary Greek woman. Accordingly, her lawlessness is not pre-*themis*; it is anti-*themis*. Having lived in civilized society, both in Colchis and in Greece, she nonetheless remains immune from those societies' most basic prescripts for human behavior. She is portrayed not as one who resists the advance into civilization, but as one who would strike at civilization's very heart to return her world to chaos.

Even worse, just as her depravity goes one step beyond that of Hesiod's iron race, she also outdoes the lawlessness of Homer's Cyclops. For, while he, in his isolation, is *without* a family, he is not represented as actively hostile to the family as an institution; it would not be inconsonant with the story as told by Homer (frivolous though it might sound) to imagine a sequel in which Polyphemus woos and wins an equally primitive wife and settles down to a harmonious family-based life with her and their offspring, following the pattern of the other Cyclopes as described by Homer in the passage quoted above (9.112–15). Medea, on the other hand, issuing from life within more than one civilized family unit (her father's, then her husband's), remains so little domesticated that she moves to destroy them from within. When Euripides has her, additionally, kill her own children—when she thus violates even the earliest and most primitive social tie, that between mother and child, the rung from which the ladder of socialization ascends—she comes to represent the total abnegation and annihilation of the social compact. Her chilling effect is rendered complete by the care the playwright takes, in presenting her to the audience, to insinuate that all her nihilistic and chaotic urges are not hers alone, but that the seeds of the disorder she embodies are in everyone: male, female; barbarian, Greek; past, present. She is the worm in the cosmos's apple.

Disorder in the play does not end, however, with the character of Medea. Just as Euripides' protagonist breeds and in the end embodies disorder, so also does the art of the play itself. Murray has said of Euripides, "He did not label half his characters bad and half good; he let both sides state their case and seemed to enjoy leaving the hearer bewildered."[2] "Bewilderment" is an appropriate term for the effect on the audience not only of Euripides' characters, but also of his plays: it connotes the loss of one's bearings, the perplexity or confusion which results from seeing no clear path to follow. To appreciate Euripides' artistry, one must further understand that the audience's bewilderment is not due to clumsy pathfinding on their part; they are able, for example, to wend their way to judgments of Sophoclean characters in whom virtues and failings mix or of pairs of characters who stand for opposite principles; they are able to appreciate shades of gray, not only black and white. Rather, Euripides, far from serving as a guide, has been deliberately removing markers, pointing ways which prove blind, and scuffing the true path over with leaves.

The *Medea* ends with an epilogue found as well at the conclusion of four other Euripidean plays:[3]

πολλῶν ταμίας Ζεὺς ἐν Ὀλύμπῳ,
πολλὰ δ᾽ ἀέλπτως κραίνουσι θεοί·
καὶ τὰ δοκηθέντ᾽ οὐκ ἐτελέσθη,
τῶν δ᾽ ἀδοκήτων πόρον ηὗρε θεός.
τοιόνδ᾽ ἀπέβη τόδε πρᾶγμα.

Zeus on Olympus is dispenser of many lots, and the gods bring about many things unlooked for. What was expected was not brought to fulfillment, and the god found a path for the unexpected. So has gone this affair.[4]

(1415-19)

Critical comments on this epilogue in the *Medea* range from acceptance of its appropriateness to the play to notation of its slight irrelevance to the preceding plot to excision of the lines as an actor's interpolation. While the lines are undoubtedly formulaic, they are, I assert, not a meaningless platitude but a concise and apt summation of a keynote of Euripidean dramaturgy. The failure of the expected to come to fruition and the achievement of the unexpected: these are surely at the heart of the *Medea*, both in plot and in theme, in the play's particular components and in its overall statement to its audience. When the Chorus turns in the play's final lines to musings on the unpredictability of life, their philosophizing may be commonplace, but their words—with clever Delphic ambiguity—apply dually as a characterization of the play's outcome and of the playwright's dramatic technique.[5] Such a sense that the epilogue has iconic significance is perhaps best reflected by an offhand, even flippant, remark by Cedric Whitman: "It is almost a commentary on himself, as well as on human life, that [Euripides] closed no less than five plays with identical choral lines stressing the unforeseeable, as if even he was not quite sure what he would do next."[6]

Euripides' purposeful achievement of the unexpected is not simply a dramatic trick, a device to create suspense and keep the audience "on the hook." It is, rather, one of the primary tools by which the poet effects the play's final chaos. To the audience that comes to him asking, " '*x*' or '*y*'?," he responds, "Not '*x*.' Nor '*y*.' " He suggests no "*z*." Worse than that, whether on the large scale or the small, he repeatedly establishes (or seems to) an either-or structure within the play, to all appearances working with "*x*'s" and "*y*'s" easily recognizable by his audience. He thus seems to be saying " '*x*' or '*y*'? I will tell you which." When he goes on to show that neither alternative is viable or true, or when the "answer" provided by the play's events is so ambiguous that the audience must conclude that the posed alternatives were simplistic or meaningless, this outcome is doubly destructive of the audience's sense of classification and order.

Right from the early lines of the prologue, it is evident that this play will be predicated on a conflict between two characters, Jason and Medea. It is equally clear that the subject of their conflict, put in the abstract, will be the Family. Within this framework, Jason is initially portrayed (by Nurse, *Paidagōgos*, and, of course, Medea) as traitor to his family; Medea is seen, conversely, as its champion. Through the murder of her children (which may itself be the single boldest stroke in the play of achieving the unexpected), Medea is revealed as the most pernicious enemy to her family, as to others'. At the same time, Jason's characterization is partially ameliorated. Yet it is obvious in the end that neither character places the value of "family" above a narrow self-interest. When these two antagonists have each proved themselves not what they initially seemed to be, the net effect is not to shift the audience's moral and sympathetic allegiance from one to the other, or even to remind them that every human personality embraces both the good and the ill, the sympathetic and the antipathetic; it is to deny outright the existence of human "good" as we would like to identify it, and of "natural" as we have always posited it.

Furthermore, within a play of conflict between two characters, it is natural to look beyond the quarreling and recriminations of two embittered people and ask what value or set of values each represents, what broader lessons we are asked to learn from their clash and its results. We can look around us every day at people whose conflicts and contacts engender passions of various types, but that is not art. The stuff of life becomes art only when an author imbues it with meaning of some sort, communicating to his audience his own interpretation of the facts and values of our world. At several points within the *Medea*, Euripides seems to be about to address such questions, proceeding from the "*x*'s" and "*y*'s" established by tradition or by other tragedians. To rehearse only a few major instances, he suggests standard antinomies between the values represented by male and female, family and state, tyrant and democrat. But he goes on to belie and befuddle each suggestion.

The summary and explication of Jason and Medea's conflict two paragraphs past is phrased in such a way as to make it as gender-neutral as possible. It tells the tale of two characters, each of whom purports to stand behind a certain value and in the end is proven not to. Euripides' play, however, is not gender-neutral. The audience is immediately alerted that this is no conflict of characters who just happen to be husband and wife, but an antithesis of the male and female sexes as their individual roles are defined (anachronistically, in respect to dramatic time) by fifth-century Athenian society. Medea identifies herself with the Chorus and calls on women's empathy; the Chorus of Corinthian women promptly grants her their allegiance, thus valuing their common gender with Medea more than their common nationality with Creon and the Corinthian royal house. Jason, on the other hand, blandly and unquestioningly assumes the superiority of his sex and undertakes a societally condoned pursuit of his masculine self-interest. The opposition of the two characters signals the audience that the outcome of the play may be expected to elucidate the rights and wrongs of their two cases and clarify the author's perspective on the male-female conflict.

The difficulties faced by those who seek such clarification from the play's ending, however, are clearly evidenced by the widely divergent perceptions at which they arrive. Suffragettes have chanted lines from Euripides' plays; generations of men have pronounced him misogynistic. Some have claimed victory for woman through Medea; others, unable to claim victory for Jason but reluctant to pronounce the child-murdering mother as victor on behalf of her own sex, have backed away from acknowledgment of the conflict's import to the play, as through assertions that Medea triumphs only as a witch or as a personification of *thumos*.

The reasons for the difficulty in assessment of Euripides' artistic intent in the play are equally obvious. Paradoxes abound. While Medea's self-identification with all women is revealed as shatteringly inappropriate as the play proceeds, there are nonetheless sinister hints that the seeds of Medea are within all women. The outcome of Medea's case does not remove from Woman the evil fame she has traditionally won from Greek poets (as the Chorus hopefully predicts), but carries it to its furthest potentiality; yet the pathos of her evocation of the helplessness of the Athenian woman among men (lines 230ff.) does not fade, nor do the polemical tones of her cry that childbirth is as great a threat to life as battle (lines 250–51). As Medea flies off in her magic chariot, she has clearly beaten Jason, but has any "cause" won? No. Just as the Chorus detaches itself from Medea once they know her true plan, but still wish Jason ill, the audience is drawn back at the end from attachment to either side.

Both characters repel, and so both sexes are indicted. The final effect is to negate the male-female conflict as originally posed: neither is right, neither wins; for both are human and thus capable of infinite depravity. Willy-nilly, the audience is forced to grapple with the intimation that, just as the play is evidently not telling the tale of one wildly atypical heroine, neither is it telling the tale simply of one sex in opposition to the other—but that Medea's actions betoken a universal potential for lawless destruction within the human soul. In a sense, at its end the *Medea is* gender-neutral.

This eventual denial of meaning to the male-female conflict is compounded by the apparent, but false, adduction at the beginning of the play of the literary tradition which identifies the conflicts between a family-based society and a government-based society with the opposition of maternalistic and paternalistic values and which symbolizes both through the dramatization of a woman and a man at odds in their most fundamental beliefs. In specific, the audience is drawn by the playwright to the expectation that in this play the causes of family and state will be joined again in the *personae* of Medea and Jason, adding another chapter to a continuing tragic discourse on the subject and resulting in some form of mediation between the characters and their values. The moral chaos effected by Medea's betrayal of her children is all the more final because this suggested symbolic structure is proved illusory, and all the audience is left with is the characters again, casting recriminations at each other without hope of mediation, neither representative of any larger value or significance; the two of them representative, in fact, of nothing except the ultimate meaninglessness of their conflict. A similarly chaotic effect is achieved both by the unexpected focus on Jason's sufferings at the end of the play, with its concomitant amelioration of his character and a resultant dislocation of the play from more normal revenge plots, and by Medea's specious adduction of a sacrificial context for the murder of her children.

Euripides' technique of "weaving to unweave" thematic antinomies extends as well to his handling of the play's civic theme. The play is structured so that Medea's debate with Jason is framed by her encounters with kings. In the first encounter, Creon renders her a third time *apolis*. In the second, Aegeus promises her refuge in Athens, reinstatement to polity. An antithesis is thus established between Corinthian and Athenian. Early indications (which would have been greeted as particularly welcome by the Athenian audience in a time of hostility between the two cities) are that this antithesis is molded in a conventional form, juxtaposing a tyrant and incipient democrat and pointing patriotically to innate Athenian superiority. Like so many other expectations, however, this one will fail to come to fruition, and the antithesis will be rendered meaningless. For, despite their initial differentiation, both kings will finally be revealed as similar: both well-meaning, properly concerned with their duty to *oikos* and *polis,* and subject to persuasion rather than rigid in mind; through these virtues, both will fall prey to Medea's manipulations, destroying (or in Aegeus's case, coming within an inch of destroying) their houses and ravaging their cities.

The effects of this revelation are complex. Medea's willingness to dupe friend as well as foe accentuates the character's moral and ethical rootlessness and shows her to be as hostile to the requirements of civic *trophē* as she is to those of familial *trophē*. At the same time, the havoc wrought or to be wrought on their cities as the result of the two kings' unwitting capitulation to Medea's deceptions points out the essential fragility of the benefits of the citizen-state compact: despite the best of will, an error in their leaders' judgment is enough to set the two cities at the mercy of Medea's particular brand of derangement. And, finally, the author's sleight of hand in whisking away traditional and apparently valid categorizations (non-Athenian tyrant, just Athenian king) contributes to a turbulent uprooting of the audience's conceptual conventions.

There is, however, an added dimension to this one failed antinomy that was absent from the others which have been discussed. Both Aegeus's initial appearance onstage and Medea's final flight to Athens involve the audience's native city in a story which otherwise might have ended where it was played out, in Corinth. Further, the foreshadowing of Medea's later attack on Theseus in Athens and the Chorus's musings on the pollution Medea will bring to Athens both, by implication, extend the play's dramatic time beyond its final act. In short, the audience is invited, in a play set in Corinth in the heroic age, to think into the future beyond dramatic time, and to think, "Athens." In a play presented in 431 B.C. and treating as one of its themes the reciprocally nurturing relationship of citizen and state, it is quite obvious that they are specifically invited to relate the events of the play in some way to contemporary Athenian political events, in particular to the impending Peloponnesian War and current Corinthian-Athenian hostility. That the Athenian audience *did* make such a connection is clear from the origin of the bribery slander related by Parmeniscus. While that charge itself is obviously absurd, the recognition which motivated it, that

Euripides was making some sort of statement about the contemporary state of Athenian political affairs, was not.

The implicit leveling of the Corinthian and Athenian kings contained in the failed tyrant-democrat antinomy runs against the current of an easy patriotism at least as vehemently as the author's failure to let the guilt for the murder of Jason and Medea's children rest with the Corinthians. Just so, the implication in the Chorus's words at lines 846ff. that the Athenians' sacred city has been polluted by Medea's entry into it cautions against an Athenian assumption of moral superiority and stirs up restless questioning of the moral and conceptual tenets on which contemporary political decisions, such as the move to war, are based.

It would be possible (and characteristic of a certain patrio-political critical tradition) to proceed from here to spin a quasi-allegorical interpretation of the *Medea*.[7] Just as Medea kills her sons to spite Jason for a failed marriage, one might say, Athens in 431 B.C. was callously threatening to send her young men off to slaughter to punish Sparta for a crumbling alliance, thus abusing her own half of the *trophē* equation, the requirement that the city nurture its young. But such a critical fabrication would be assailable not only for over-interpretation, but for coarsening the allusive texture of Euripides' thematic web. Euripides does not raise questions in his audience's minds and subvert the tenets of their conceptual world in order to answer them with a single, simplistic allegorical message. Nor does he do so to be anti-patriotic. Euripides will not allow his audience even the cold comfort of knowing that he is arguing an opposite point. His effect is at once subtler and more diffuse.

By interweaving the threads of familial and civic *trophē* into Medea's story, Euripides has presented his audience with a protagonist whose actions are relentlessly hostile to the *nomoi brotōn* which many would like to think of as absolute and to the social compact which is built on that substructure, and further with a dramatic world in which every given may be taken away. Lest his audience sit back and presume that such things may happen only onstage, or only in the mythic past, or only when wrought by a barbarian witch, the allusive insertion of Athens into the play intimates that the confusion Medea embodies lives on to the present day and touches them even on their sacred citadel, for it is part of the human condition. They are propelled to examine the underpinnings of heretofore unexamined conceptual frameworks, to reflect upon the failures of all human compacts, and finally to gaze upon Medea's lawlessness among and in themselves. To paraphrase Collard (see note 7), they are invited to illuminate their Athenian microcosm by reference to the macrocosm depicted in the play.

To what end did Euripides create and instill in his audience this sense of cosmic chaos? The *Medea* is nihilistic in that its protagonist brings to nothing the very cornerstones of human order and that the play itself brings to nothing its audience's attempts at ordering, conceptually, its dramatic world and threatens to do the same to the world they live in. But was he himself a nihilist in the sense that he professed the essential meaninglessness of human life? Or, in the sophistic tradition, did he assume that old truths must be revealed as truisms and then destroyed? Was he, to any degree, consciously performing the preparatory function along the road to truth of dragging his audience out of the cave into the blinding sunlight, where all judgment must necessarily, for the moment, be dazzled? Pucci goes one step further, to assert that Euripides' "metaphysical aim" was therapeutic:

> The painful experience that each member of the audience suffers as he is exposed to the force of Euripides' discourse turns into a serene contemplation of beauty and the recognition of his own wisdom. The violence we behold and dread in the course of the action is somehow lifted and replaced by the sense of our own peace and *charis*.[8]

But Pucci also notes myriad ways in which Euripides' own language works against the aim Pucci attributes to him and thus "questions its success."[9] It is thus that one critical tradition approaches and analyzes the confusions engendered by the tangle of characterizations, plot elements, and themes that a Euripidean play presents. By contrast, the critical stance adopted in this study has been to presume that Euripides aimed at just the kind of anomaly and confusion he achieved.

But we are not, finally, meant to know—no more than we are meant to leave the *Medea* with a satisfactory sense of closure. Bewilderment, ambivalence, fear: these are some of the responses Euripides demands from his audience. But he will not return what we so inherently ask of an author: the sense that, with sufficient concentration, we may grasp his meaning. We leave the text, as the audience must have left the theater, disquieted and unsure. Τοιόνδ' ἀπέβη τόδε πρᾶγμα.

Notes

Introduction

1. Two studies which appeared in the same year amply demonstrate, through specific comparison to Sophocles' *Ajax* and through numerous elements of language, action, and dramatic structure, Medea's presentation to the audience in the mold of a classic Sophoclean hero. These are Bernard Knox, "The *Medea* of Euripides," *YCS* 25 (1977), 174ff., hereafter cited as reprinted in B. Knox, *Word and Action: Essays on the Ancient Theater* (Johns Hopkins Press, Baltimore, 1979), 295ff.; and Elizabeth Bryson Bongie, "Heroic Elements in the *Medea* of Euripides," *TAPA* 107 (1977), 27–56.

2. Knox, *W. & A.*, 330.

3. Bernard Knox, "Euripides: The Poet as Prophet," in Peter Burian, ed., *Directions in Euripidean Criticism: A Collection of Essays* (Duke University Press, Durham, 1985), 2.

4. Knox (1985), 8.

5. Pietro Pucci, *The Violence of Pity in Euripides' Medea* (Cornell University Press, Ithaca and London, 1980), 17.

6. William Arrowsmith, in the preface to his translation of the *Orestes* in the Grene-Lattimore series (*Euripides IV* [University of Chicago Press, Chicago and London, 1958], 106), places this characterization of the play in quotation marks but does not locate the reference. Whether they are his own words or someone else's, they express admirably the atmosphere of the play.

7. The critical ire provoked by the magic chariot (after Medea's portrayal in resolutely human terms) provides a single telling example; see, e.g., Norwood, as cited in ch. 3, n. 4; cp. Eilhard Schlesinger, "Zu Euripides *Medea*," *Hermes* 94 (1966), 33, on the generality of this ire. A lovely antidote is con-

120   Notes

tained in N. E. Collinge's brief discussion, "Medea *Ex Machina*," *CP* 57 (1962), 170–72.

8. Vladimir Nabokov, *Speak Memory* (New York, 1966), 290; quoted in Robert Eisner, "Euripides' Use of Myth," *Arethusa* 12 (1979), 153.

9. Anne P. Burnett, *Catastrophe Survived: Euripides' Plays of Mixed Reversal* (Oxford University Press, Oxford, 1971); cp. Burnett, "*Medea* and the Tragedy of Revenge," *CP* 68:1 (1973), 1–24 (see esp. pp. 69–70 and ch. 4, n. 10 below).

10. All the Euripidean exegeses in *W. & A.*, as well as Knox (1985), contain examples. Knox's term "deformation" is from his review of Burnett (1971), which originally appeared in *CP* 66:4 (1972) and is reprinted in *W. & A.*, 329–42, the relevant passage from which is quoted below, ch. 2, n. 27.

11. Eisner, 153–74.

12. Richard Hamilton, "Prologue, Prophecy and Plot in Four Plays of Euripides," *AJP* 99:3 (1978), 277–302.

13. R. P. Winnington-Ingram, "Euripides: *Poiētēs Sophos*," *Arethusa* 2:2 (1969), 127–42; Geoffrey Arnott, "Euripides and the Unexpected," *G. & R.* 20 (1973), 49–64; cp. Arnott, "Red Herrings and Other Baits, A Study in Euripidean Techniques," *MPL* 3 (1978), 1–24; F. J. Nisetich, "The Silencing of Pylades (*Orestes* 1591–1592)," *AJP* 107 (1986), 46–54.

14. Rick M. Newton, "Ino in Euripides' *Medea*," *AJP* 106 (1985), 496–502.

15. T. V. Buttrey, "Accident and Design in Euripides' *Medea*," *AJP* 79:1 (1958), 1–17.

16. Buttrey, 1–17.

17. Bongie, 29 and 29 n. 9; P. E. Easterling, "The Infanticide in Euripides' *Medea*," *YCS* 25 (1977), 181 and 186.

18. Alan Elliott, *Euripides: Medea* (Oxford University Press, London, 1969), see esp. 117–18.

19. To deny that the child-murder is the dramatic focus of the play takes a great (and artificial) effort of critical will and ingenuity (see pp. 25–26, for example, for discussion of such an effort by one particular critic). Such efforts are born of an impulse to "normalize" the grotesque happenings onstage; they distort the critic's appreciation of the play.

20. See, e.g., Knox, *W. & A.*, esp. 306ff.; Philip Vellacott, *Ironic Drama: A Study of Euripides' Method and Meaning* (Cambridge University Press, London, 1975), esp. 106ff.; A. Dihle, "Euripides' Medea und ihre Schwestern im europäischen Drama," *A. & A.* 22 (1976), 175–84; Kenneth J. Reckford, "Medea's First Exit," *TAPA* 99 (1968), 339; Pucci, 61ff.

Chapter 1

1. Examples abound. A small sample of major and minor innovations which can with some certainty be attributed to Euripides includes the guilty verdict pronounced by the Argive jury of the *Or.* (in an ironic inversion of the Athenian trial scene of Aeschylus's *Eum.*); his *El.*'s inclusion of Electra in the madness which traditionally besets her brother only and, in the same play, Electra's unconsummated marriage; and Orestes' ambush of Neoptolemus in the *Andr.* Innovations in Euripides are frequently negative in the sense that they are tied with character degeneration and a concomitant downturn in

assessment of human nature; for a discussion of this latter phenomenon, see Emily A. McDermott, "Euripides and the Decline of Character: A Soap Opera Connection," *The Classical Outlook* 61:4 (May/June, 1984), 105–8, and below, pp. 41f.

2. Accounts of the various sources and their implications may be found in Louis Séchan, *Études sur la Tragédie Grecque dans ses Rapports avec la Céramique* (Champion, Paris, 1926), Appendix VI, 589–91 (a valuable source of bibliography); in *RE*, s.v. *Medeia*, col. 41ff.; in Denys L. Page, *Euripides, Medea* (Oxford University Press, Oxford, 1938), xxiff.; in D. J. Conacher, *Euripidean Drama: Myth, Theme and Structure* (University of Toronto Press, Toronto, 1967), 184ff.; and in Louis Méridier et al., eds., *Euripide I*, Budé edition (Paris, 1947), 105–10; cp. Schlesinger, 39ff.

3. In discussing the type and degree of originality available to the poets in treating received myth, Aristotle states that, while they cannot change the basic facts (like Clytemnestra's death at Orestes' hands), they do have leeway to interpret the facts to the best effect. He then cites as examples the contrast between the unwitting sins of Sophocles' Oedipus and the deliberate crimes of Euripides' Medea: ἔστι μὲν γὰρ οὕτω γίνεσθαι τὴν πρᾶξιν, ὥσπερ οἱ παλαιοὶ ἐποίουν εἰδότας καὶ γιγνώσκοντας, καθάπερ καὶ Εὐριπίδης ἐποίησεν ἀποκτείνουσαν τοὺς παῖδας τὴν Μήδειαν: "The deed of horror may be done by the doer knowingly and consciously, as in the old poets and in Medea's murder of her children in Euripides" (tr. Ingram Bywater, Aristotle, *On the Art of Poetry* [Clarendon Press, Oxford, 1909]). Critics (e.g., Séchan) who cite this passage as a deterrent to Wilamowitz's thesis of spontaneous mythic innovation apparently assume (and with a measure of verisimilitude) that the Aristotelian *exemplum* is predicated on the presumption that in earlier versions of the myth the element of deliberate murder by the mother was absent. This is not, however, an inescapable inference, for the primary point of Aristotle's example is plainly not to contrast Euripides' character with earlier Medeas, but to contrast the three types of plot-line available to the tragedian: those involving (a) purposeful sin; (b) inadvertent sin; and (c) narrowly averted sin.

4. Page, xxiv.

5. Notable subscribers to this view include Buttrey, Conacher, Knox.

6. Séchan, 589.

7. Walter Burkert, "Greek Tragedy and Sacrificial Ritual," *GRBS* 7:2 (1966), 118 n. 71; see his discussion, 118–19.

8. Pucci, 133.

9. Helene P. Foley, *Ritual Irony: Poetry and Sacrifice in Euripides* (Cornell University Press, Ithaca, 1985), 22: "Medea's violent sacrifice of her sons becomes rationalized in the harmless repetition of the children's cult at Corinth." The contrary view is accorded no mention.

10. Newton, 501, counterbalances Foley (n. 9) by presenting the Page-ian orthodoxy as an unchallenged premise: "For it is well-known that the plot of the play [the *Medea*] revolves around a shocking change in the mythological tradition: Euripides is the first to present Medea as the deliberate murderess of her sons."

11. The evidence is summarized in Séchan, 396ff. While Burkert, 118, cites as support of his theory that "vase-paintings constantly show Medea killing

her children at an altar," this unadorned statement is not sufficient to counter the critical fact that no artistic portrayals of Medea at Corinth predate the end of the fifth century and Page's detailed arguments (lviiff.: with others [see Séchan]) that nothing in them necessitates a conclusion that they draw on a separate and pre-Euripidean mythic tradition concerning the murder of the children.

12. On the cult at Corinth, see *Med.* 1381–83; Séchan, 590; Burkert (1966), 118–19.

13. See Séchan, 590–91 and ch. 3, n. 5; feasible assessment of the relation between the various versions of the myth and the cult at Corinth obviously rests partially on (and varies with) the question of whether Medea was originally an early tutelary divinity of Corinth or merely the wife of a hero who sought refuge from exile there.

14. Schol. *Med.* 8; cp. Ael., *VH* 5.21; see discussion in Page, xxv (cp. xxxi). The translation is Page's: on the translation of the *apax legomenon poluaikos* ("much-rushing") as "widespread" (as opposed to *LSJ*'s "impetuous"), see Page, xxv, n. 2.

15. For a useful review of the issues, the varied approaches to them, and the secondary literature which treats them (from both anthropological and literary points of view), see Foley's first chapter, 17–64. Among those whose approach to the connection between tragedy and sacrifice is primarily literary are Pucci, Foley, and Froma I. Zeitlin, "The Motif of the Corrupted Sacrifice in Aeschylus' *Oresteia*," *TAPA* 96 (1965), 463–508; ———, "Postscript to the Sacrificial Imagery in the *Oresteia* (*Ag.* 1235–37)," *TAPA* 97 (1966), 645–53; ——— ———, "The Argive Festival of Hera and Euripides' *Electra*," *TAPA* 101 (1970), 645–49. For discussion of Medea's assumption of a sacrificial metaphor for the murder of her children (*Med.* 1053–55), see below, pp. 74ff.

16. Burkert, 118.

17. That it may be so taken is asserted directly by Pietro Pucci, "Euripides: The Monument and the Sacrifice," *Arethusa* (Spring, 1977), 166, and is the fundamental underlying principle of his work and of others who write on the connection between literature and sacrifice.

18. Foley, 60. For further discussion, see also 17ff., 35–46, 57–64.

19. Pucci, 131ff. See esp. 132–33.

20. See esp. 133–35.

21. Although Pucci does not specifically address the issues surrounding the question of innovation, his judgment on this matter should not be dismissed lightly. Let me then address for a moment the particular use to which Pucci puts Burkert's postulate. After accepting the traditionality of the child-murder argued by Burkert, Pucci sums up: "The saga of Medea's murder is the mythical elaboration of a ceremony emphasizing, through sacrifice, a time of crisis, destruction, and new beginning, the breaking of the old order and the recomposition of a new order" (133). He goes on to expound his view that the assumption of a sacrificial metaphor was intended by Euripides "to attribute purifying and remedial force to his play" (135) (much as sacrificial ritual was aimed at purification and remediation); at the same time he points to the subversion of this authorial intention by the imperfection of the parallelism asserted by the metaphor. While this critical construct is obviously stronger if Euripides' sacrificial metaphor would be heard by the audience as reflective of

a known mythic aetiology for the cult of Hera Acraea "established" at the end of the play (1381–83), it does not stand or fall with that tenet, for the same parallelism might be asserted even by the unexpected evocation by the character of a sacrificial context for her proposed slayings. At a later point in this study I shall voice skepticism of Pucci's overall sense of the ultimately uplifting effects of this play and of Euripides' art in general (see p. 118); here it will suffice to say, in bringing argumentation concerning the innovation or traditionality of the child-murder to a close, that one must be wary of laying such credence in any complex critical construct (even a plausible one) which is in turn predicated on an uncertain tenet of fact as to then decide on the basis of the plausibility of the construct that the questionable fact must be true.

22. One of these points has previously been presented, though via a somewhat different line of argumentation from that which will be offered here, in Emily A. McDermott, "*Medea* Line 37: A Note," *AJP* 108:1 (Spring, 1987), 158–61.

23. Winnington-Ingram, 131ff.

24. E.g., Arnott, Nisetich (Intro., n. 13).

25. For further discussion of these lines in their context, see below, pp. 33ff.

26. Page, *ad loc.*

27. Rex Warner, tr., Euripides, *Medea*, in *Complete Greek Tragedies*, vol. I (University of Chicago Press, Chicago, 1955), *ad loc.*

28. It is suggestive that *apallassō* is compounded from *allassō* ("exchange"); Euripides changes the old version for the new.

29. E.g., *Med.* 1378ff., *Heracl.* 1026ff., *Hipp.* 1423ff., *IT* 1449ff., *IA* 1467ff., *Alc.* 1154ff., et al. See J. C. Kamerbeek, "Mythe et réalité dans l'oeuvre d'Euripide," *Entretiens sur l'antiquité classique* 6 (Fondation Hardt, Geneva, 1958), 1–41; Cedric Whitman, "Euripides and the Full Circle of Myth" (Harvard University Press, Cambridge, 1974), 118–19; Foley, 21ff.

30. On Neophron, see citations and discussions in Séchan, Appendix VII, 592–94; Albin Lesky, *Die tragische Dichtung der Hellenen*³ (Gottingen, 1956), 301; Page, xxxff.; Conacher, 186 n. 5; Knox, W. & A., 316–17 n. 7. As E. A. Thompson has summarized in his 1944 espousal of Neophron's anteriority, "Neophron and Euripides' *Medea*," *CQ* 30:1,2 (1944), 10–14: "Neophron's priority has been maintained by Weil, Bergk, Decharme, Haigh [*sic*: A. E. Haigh, *The Tragic Drama of the Greeks* (Clarendon Press, Oxford, 1896, 290–91 and 418), though he does set Neophron in the fifth century, remains carefully neutral on the subject of priority], Croiset, Norwood, etc.; Euripides' by Paley, Wilamowitz, Nauck, Christ-Schmid, Séchan, Méridier, and many others. The latter have predominated in recent times" (10 n. 2). It should be added that, while Thompson's own exegesis has, to my knowledge, won several supporters (in print, see, e.g., Richard Hamilton, "Required Readings: Euripides," *New England Classical Newsletter*, vol. xv: 2 [December, 1987], 16), the preponderance of published response has continued the trend of favoring Euripidean anteriority.

31. The two later sources attribute a more blanket plagiarism to Euripides but are themselves less elaborated than the charge in the Hypothesis: (a) πταίουσιν οἱ λέγοντες μηδὲν αὐτὸν ἀνεγνωκέναι πλὴν τῆς Μηδείας τῆς Εὐριπίδου, ἣν ἔνιοι Νεόφρονος εἶναι τοῦ Σικυωνίου φασίν: "Those who say that he [sc. Menedemus] had read nothing but Euripides' *Medea* (which some

say is by Neophron of Sicyon) are mistaken" (Diog. Laert. 2.134); (b) Νεόφρων . . . Σικυώνιος· οὗ φασὶν εἶναι τὴν τοῦ Εὐριπίδου Μήδειαν· ὃς πρῶτος εἰσήγαγε παιδαγωγοὺς καὶ οἰκετῶν βάσανον: "Neophron of Sicyon: they say Euripides' *Medea* was by him; he was the first to bring *paidagōgoi* and the torture of slaves into drama" (Suda, s.v. Νεόφρων).

32. They issue, respectively, from Schol. Eur. *Med.* 666, Stob. Flor. 20.34, and Schol. Eur. *Med.* 1387; they are available, e.g., in Nauck, 729–32, and Page, xxxii–xxxiii.

33. Summarized by Thompson, 14.

34. Séchan, 593.

35. For arguments that the Aegeus episode in Euripides is *not* embarrassingly unmotivated, see ch. 5, n. 9 and discussions in chs. 5–6.

36. Thompson, 14.

Chapter 2

1. Page, xiv–xv.

2. If this element were somehow incidental or unnecessary to true appreciation of the play, one might ask Page (who argues forcefully that the deliberate child-murder was Euripides' own innovation) why Euripides then chose to add it to a myth in which it had played no previous part. For the critic who declines to accept the child-murder as innovation, one might rephrase this question, with almost as much point, to ask why Euripides then chose to adopt this most shocking version of the myth, with its concomitant acquittal of the Corinthians.

3. This and subsequent references from the *Eth. Nic.* appear as translated by H. Rackham, Aristotle, *The Nicomachean Ethics* (Harvard University Press, Cambridge, 1934), The Loeb Classical Library.

4. Beginning at *Eth. Nic.* 8.12.1 (1161^b), Aristotle cites several arguments to explain the tenets he posits, that parents' love for their children is more natural, intense, long-standing, and abiding than the converse; at 8.14.4 (1163^b), after intervening discussion of related issues, he glosses his conclusion that a father may with legitimacy disown his son (but the son may not repudiate his father) with another glance at the societal system of *trophē* (here referred to by the word *epikouria:* "aid, succor"):

ἅμα δ᾽ ἴσως οὐδείς ποτ᾽ ἂν ἀποστῆναι δοκεῖ μὴ ὑπερβάλλοντος μοχθηρίᾳ· χωρὶς γὰρ τῆς φυσικῆς φιλίας τὴν ἐπικουρίαν ἀνθρωπικὸν μὴ διωθεῖσθαι. τῷ δὲ φευκτὸν ἢ οὐ σπουδαστὸν τὸ ἐπαρκεῖν, μοχθηρῷ ὄντι· εὖ πάσχειν γὰρ οἱ πολλοὶ βούλονται, τὸ δὲ ποιεῖν φεύγουσιν ὡς ἀλυσιτελές.

At the same time, no doubt it is unlikely that a father ever would abandon a son unless the son were excessively vicious; for natural affection apart, it is not in human nature to reject that assistance (*epikourian*) that a son will be able to render, whereas a bad son will look on the duty of supporting his father as one to be avoided, or at all events not eagerly undertaken; for most people wish to receive benefits, but avoid bestowing them as unprofitable.

5. See, e.g., *Med.* 187–88, Callim. *Cer.* 50–52, Ovid *Ars Am.* 2.375 (of lions); Hom. *Od.* 20.14–15, Sem. 7 (Diehl). 33–34 (of dogs); Soph. *Ant.* 423–25 (of birds).

6. The translation is from the Loeb text: E. C. Marchant, tr., Xenophon, *Memorabilia and Oeconomicus* (Heinemann, London; G. P. Putnam, New York; 1923).

7. On the provenance of punishment for breach of oaths, see Walter Burkert, *Greek Religion*, tr., John Raffan (Harvard University Press, Cambridge, 1985), 252: "The ordinary man believes that Zeus hurls his thunderbolt against perjurers, even if this is not confirmed by experience. Speculation therefore discovers subterranean law officers who punish oath-breakers in the underworld after death; Hesiod warns that the oath, even as it is born, is surrounded by Erinyes." All these imagined forthcoming retributions emphasize the fact that there is really not much in the present practical world to prevent an oath-taker from committing perjury, nor is there much practical recourse against him if he does. On the presumption of widespread breach of oaths from early Greek times on, see Burkert, 253. It is especially pertinent in Jason's case to note, with Burkert (446 n. 44), the "wise maxim 'Demand no oath in matters of love' " (Hes. fr. 124=Apollod. 2.5). By contrast, Burnett (1973), 12ff., argues eloquently that Jason's breach of oaths is his primary crime and the primary symptom of the moral corruption at the heart of the play. I agree that lost respect for oaths is a notable thematic element within the play (see, e.g., pp. 102ff., on *both* Jason and Medea as oath-breakers); but to view Jason as Oath-Breaker writ large, with symbolic significance, puts excess credence in Medea's version of events (Jason—if he had even chosen to defend himself on this charge—would undoubtedly have seen these same "oaths" as lovers' promises, written on wind or water) and invests too much weight in what is surely only one of many symptoms in the play of pervasive moral failure.

8. Philip Slater, *The Glory of Hera* (Beacon Press, Boston, 1968), bases many observations throughout his study on such a view of the mother-son relationship in Athens.

9. See, e.g., the summary assessment of Slater's work by Sarah B. Pomeroy, "Selected Bibliography on Women in Antiquity," *Arethusa* 6:1 (1973), 137–38.

10. Easterling, 186–87.

11. Page, xx–xxi. Knox, W. & A., 309ff., argues "irrelevant to the problems of Greek society." Easterling similarly inquires, "If Medea is to be seen as a distinctively oriental type . . . why does Euripides make her talk like a Greek, argue like a Greek, and to all appearances *feel* like a Greek?" (Easterling, 180).

12. Somewhat like the Greek settings of Roman comedy, they offer the audience only a partial "out" from full-fledged adoption as their own of the events and behavior onstage.

13. Reckford, 339. For similar views that Medea's actions have universal implications, see also the other sources cited in Intro., n. 20.

14. Knox, W. & A., 310, neatly turns on Page his assertion that a typically barbarian (as opposed to Greek) cruelty is exemplified by Astyages' having, in Page's words, "set a Thyestean feast before Harpagos." "But," Knox contin-

ues, "the adjective 'Thyestean' gives the game away—that's a *Greek* story!—and the list of Persian atrocities which follows contains nothing which cannot be paralleled, or for that matter bettered, from Greek myth and history."

15. If I may be permitted a parenthetical lament, as a teacher of Greek literature in translation: a whole new generation of readers (who so often, these days, come to the classics as veritable *tabulae rasae*) have their experience of this play shaped by the brief introduction to Rex Warner's translation in the Grene-Lattimore University of Chicago series. This introduction informs the new reader that "the Athenian audience would know well enough what the plot would be," listing, among other "well-known" elements, the mother's willful murder of her children. Given what some see as a likelihood, and others would admit to be at least a possibility—that ancient viewers were in fact to be stunned by the realization that such a crime would transpire at the end of the play—then modern readers should be given the opportunity to experience this realization in the same way.

16. Euripides' first entry at the Dionysia in 455 had included his *Peliades*. The date of his *Aegeus* is unknown; Knox, *W. & A.*, 316 n. 5, argues against the seeming consensus that it must predate the *Med.*; but the story of Medea in Athens was part of received myth at the time of the *Med.*'s production (see ch. 5, n. 10).

17. For a detailed discussion of the textual problems that vex lines 38ff., see Page, *ad loc.* Page tentatively follows Dindorf's deletion of 38–43. While the resultant omission of all reference here to violence against the newly married couple (40–42) would make the anticipated direction of Medea's vengeful temper less explicit, lines 44–45 still make it clear that the Nurse envisions the burden as falling upon those whose actions have incurred Medea's enmity (οὔτοι ῥαδίως γε συμβαλὼν / ἔχθραν τις αὐτῇ καλλίνικον οἴσεται : "A person who joins enmity with her will not easily carry off the glory of victory"). Such a characterization obviously is not suited to Medea's children.

18. Creon's daughter is not named in Euripides' play. I will on occasion call her "Creusa" (the more neutral of the two names ascribed to her by later writers) as a narrative convenience. "Creusa" (like "Creon," the masculine form of the same word: i.e., "ruling one") was a stock name for a princess/ queen; the other name later attributed to the Corinthian princess was Glauce.

19. The possibility of a sophisticated double entendre hidden in this first foreshadowing has been discussed above, pp. 17ff.

20. The emphatic development of the "children-theme" is traced, e.g., by G. M. A. Grube, *The Drama of Euripides* (Methuen, London, 1973; 1st pub., 1941), 148–50.

21. While there are serious difficulties with the text of line 183 (Page, *ad loc.*), the sense of the line is nonetheless clear, as Page notes, following Elmsley: "Propera tu priusquam aliquid mali faciat Medea": "You, hurry before Medea does something bad."

22. Most critics note the change (see discussion, e.g., at Pucci, 197 n. 1); Conacher (188; cp. 35) suggests an interesting comparison with Phaedra's first appearance in the *Hipp.*

23. Given what the audience knows about Medea's powers with magical herbs (and her unscrupulousness in using them) from her mythic biography and from the Nurse's brief allusion to the murder of Pelias at lines 9–10, her

lament to Creon that her "intelligence" has created an unfair prejudice against her (292ff.) takes on something of the nature of a sinister euphemism. Similarly, Medea's account of her plight at lines 255–58 is carefully expurgated to omit details prejudicial to her—a fact which might inspire in her audience an early sense of her disingenuousness. The irony of her saddened reflection that she has neither mother nor brother to turn to for help has quite properly elicited from Page the remark: "the coolness of ἀδελφόν ['brother'] 257 is perfectly shocking—what did she do with her brother when she *had* one?" (at 231).

24. The question naturally arises as to exactly when Medea herself arrives at her plan. Gilbert Murray, tr., *Medea* (G. Allen, London, 1906), 90 (cp. H. Darnley Naylor, "The Aegeus Episode," *Medea* 663–773," CR 23 [1909], 189–90), followed by Page, xxix–xxx, and many others (e.g., Bongie, 40ff.), asserts that she made up her mind only during—and as a result of—the Aegeus-episode. This theory rests on the assumption that it is the sight of Aegeus's desperation at his own persistent childlessness that suggests to Medea the fiendish idea of reducing Jason to the same state. This theory is neat and in many ways appealing: one can almost see a lightbulb going off over Medea's head as she hears in her own words to Aegeus (ἄπαις γὰρ δεῦρ᾽ ἀεὶ τείνεις βίον;: "Do you still to this day carry your life on childless (*apais*)?" [670]) an echo of her earlier complaint to Jason that his betrayal of her was completely unjustified: εἰ γὰρ ἦσθ᾽ ἄπαις ἔτι, / συγγνώστ᾽ ἂν ἦν σοι τοῦδ᾽ ἐρασθῆναι λέχους: "For, if you were still childless (*apais*), your longing for this new bed would be pardonable" (490–91). On the other hand, Euripides never confirms that a previously undefined urge for revenge takes on definite shape only here, and one may be pardoned if, with Conacher, one tends to the suspicion that "Medea has from the start been determined on this course of action" (Conacher, 192; he elaborates on his demurral from Page on this point at 190 n. 11). This critic, for one, before reading Page, Murray, *or* Conacher, had always assumed that Medea's plan was fixed in her own mind right from her first entrance onto the stage, and that her announcement at 374–75 that her vengeance would fall on Jason, Creon, and the princess was a deliberate red herring, intended by Medea to deceive the Chorus and by Euripides to lull his audience into suspicionlessness concerning the children. In support of this interpretation, it may be noted that, when Medea reveals her true plan to the Chorus immediately after Aegeus's exit from the stage (764ff.), she does not say, "Now I know how to get my revenge," but "Now I shall tell you (λέξω) my plans in their entirety (πάντα τἀμά . . . βουλεύματα [772])"; to those who might ask why she would dissemble at the beginning of the play only to tell all at line 792, one may respond that (a) on the level of plot and character, it was only prudent for Medea to remain vague until the ironing out of the final detail, her escape, rendered her plan perfect and, so, fixed; the Chorus's scandalized response when they do discover her full plan proves the point of her initial prudence: could she have counted on their continued complicity if they had known all along (especially when Creon and Jason were onstage) that she planned the unnatural murder of her own sons? And (b) on the level of authorial intent, her dissembling was critical to achievement of the requisite level of suspense in Euripides' audience. Either inference concerning the time of her decision, however, seems feasible; conversely, neither is sure (cp.

Easterling, 185–86; Elliott at lines 374–75 and 671), and one begins to suspect that uncertainty is exactly the state of mind Euripides intended to arouse in us. As so often, he deliberately afflicts us with doubts. Once we find out what Medea truly plans and will in fact carry out, we naturally look back, in mind, to her earlier words and actions, for it would be only by pinpointing her moment of decision that we could come to any sure judgment, retrospectively, of her character. Surely she is *worse* if she can cold-bloodedly manipulate Creon into giving her a day's grace by feigning maternal protectiveness for the children she already plans to kill. Euripides, however, will not permit his audience even a retrospective sense that at least *now* they know for sure what she was like; they are forced to remain suspended in a state of doubt.

25. Conacher, 189 and 192, notes some ways in which the "children theme" is kept "before our minds"; cp. Grube, 148ff.

26. McDermott (1984), 107.

27. In this assertion, I differ from Gilbert Murray, *Euripides and His Age* (Oxford University Press, London, 1946; originally published 1913), 135–36. In his general discussion of the Euripidean prologue, Murray assumes that tragic irony is a universal working principle; he does not differentiate between Sophocles and Euripides, nor between the *Med.* and the *Hipp.*:

> Why does it spoil the excitement beforehand? Because, we must answer, there is no secret, and the poet does not aim at that sort of excitement. A certain amount of plot-interest there certainly is: we are never told exactly what thing will happen but only what sort of thing; or we are told what will happen but not how it will happen. But the enjoyment which the poet aims at is not the enjoyment of reading a detective story for the first time; it is that of reading *Hamlet* or *Paradise Lost* for the second or fifth or tenth. When Hippolytus or Oedipus first appears on the stage you know that he is doomed; that knowledge gives an increased significance to everything that he says or does; you see the shadow of disaster closing in behind him, and when the catastrophe comes it comes with the greater force because you were watching for it.

In the *Med.*, however, as in certain later plays (e.g., perhaps most notably, the *Or.*; one might mention as well the *Andr.*), Euripides has adopted a different working principle. Knox characterizes this difference well when he speaks of Euripides' "deformations" of plot and character:

> The irony of situation which Sophocles exploits with such demonic expertise, playing on the audience's knowledge of the outcome to invest his character's ignorant pronouncements with tragic significance, becomes in Euripides an irony of form, which poses the all-too-human motives and actions of the characters against the audience's expectations of the required heroic tone and counts on their familiarity with the conventional tragic plots and roles to ensure appreciation of his deformations, ranging from subtle to outrageous, of the norms. (*W. & A.*, 330)

Of course, this is not to say that Euripides' literary bag of tricks does not include the use of standard tragic irony as well. The approaching doom of Pentheus in the *Bacch.*, as he seeks to overmaster the Stranger and to disprove the divinity of Dionysus, to cite a single example, is played out along a classic principle of tragic irony. Even within the overall linear revelation of plot in the *Med.*, tragic irony has its place: the extremely pathetic effect of the second scene between Jason and Medea (866ff.), in which Medea convinces Jason that she has come to her senses and accepted the wisdom of his actions, results from the audience's awareness (after her announcement at 792–93) that Jason's rosy projections for his sons' future are blindly misguided (see pp. 52f.).

Chapter 3

1. See, e.g., A. Lesky, *Die Griechische Tragödie* (Stüttgart, Leipzig, 1958), 147–48; Conacher, 186; H. D. F. Kitto, *Greek Tragedy*[3] (Methuen & Co., London, 1961), 200–201; Knox, *W. & A.*, 306ff.; R. A. Browne, "*Medea*-Interpretations," in Mary White, ed., *Studies in Honour of Gilbert Norwood* (University of Toronto Press, Toronto, 1952), 77–79; Reckford, 329ff.; Schlesinger, 33–35.

2. My arguments in the next few pages are related, in overall viewpoint and on occasion in choice of supporting evidence, to Knox's treatment, *W. & A.*, 306ff.

3. There is necessarily a distinct element of anachronism here, since the "times" of Medea and Euripides are separated by approximately a thousand years, as well as a glossing over of the geographical/cultural distinction between Athens and Corinth. Yet this blurring merely enhances the sense of anomaly so essential to the play; we need not, with Norwood and others less extreme than he, regret the failure in iron-clad logic.

4. Gilbert Norwood, *Essays on Euripidean Drama* (University of California Press, Berkeley; Cambridge University Press, London; University of Toronto Press, Toronto; 1954), 34, voices an uneasiness shared by many others when he notes: "So momentous a resource [as the magic chariot] clashes ruinously with the repeated assertion of Medea's helpless situation." But it is an integral part of the artistry of this play that everyday womanhood and demonic power are made to dwell in uneasy alliance within a single character. Because he does not recognize the artistic potential of the anomaly (which figures so centrally in this play's techniques), Norwood is driven to the outlandish conclusion that the *Med.* as we have it represents a core play of infinitely better and evener quality, originally presented "at a private performance in Aspasia's house or Agathon's or his own" (33) but later padded out to the requisite length for presentation at the Dionysia.

5. There is no mention in the mythic sources of Medea's death. Like Helen, Pasiphae, Ariadne, she may be an example of a "faded" goddess. Walter Burkert, *Structure and History in Greek Mythology and Ritual*, Sather Classical Lectures 47 (University of California Press, Berkeley, 1979), 9–10, and 148 nn. 27–29, who asserts positively her divine status, draws an intriguing parallel between the Jason/Medea-saga and Hittite mythology. For bibliography concerning the possibility that she was an early tutelary divinity of Corinth, see Séchan, 590–91; cp. ch. 1, n. 13.

6. Pucci, 37–38.

7. See 31ff., 166–67, 328, 431, 441ff., 502–3, 643ff., 798ff., 1332; cp. 257.

8. In my assertion, I differ from Easterling, 180–81, in two ways. First, I

do not agree that Euripides is here vague about the legalities, relying on the setting of the play in the heroic age. Concubinage was always legal. And while at the time the *Med.* was actually produced Pericles' citizenship law of 451–450 was in effect, providing that only those born of citizen mothers could be Athenian citizens, the looser regulations were well within Euripides' (and much of his audience's) memory; if Euripides relied on the setting of the play in the past, he had to go back only twenty years to reach a time when Jason's plan of joining his children by the princess with his children by Medea into one big happy citizen family would have been still possible in Athens. Second, Jason's stated plan belies Easterling's assertion that no one in the play suggests that Medea's legal status as foreigner is relevant to Jason's plans. With Easterling, however, I dispute the assertion in Murray (1906), vii–viii, 81, that as a foreigner Medea was not Jason's legitimate wife in the first place.

9. See esp. 359ff., 387–90, 712–13, 768–69.

10. Page, xxiv. For the *Med.*'s use of the traditional mythic motif exemplified by Ino/Procne, see S. P. Mills, "The Sorrows of Medea," *CP* 75:4 (1980), 289–96; which in turn proceeds from J. Fontenrose, "The Sorrows of Ino and of Procne," *TAPA* 79 (1948), 125–67; for the *Med.*, see esp. 131, 159, 165. Newton's more recent analysis (see Intro., n. 14) has important insights to add. Paradoxically, an assertion that the child-murder motif is grafted onto the Medea-saga by deliberate analogy with the story of Procne derives support from the seemingly perplexing fact that the Chorus of Euripides' *Med.* fails to mention Procne when they try to think of precedents for Medea's untoward action:

μίαν δὴ κλύω μίαν τῶν πάρος
γυναῖκ' ἐν φίλοις χέρα βαλεῖν τέκνοις·
Ἰνὼ μανεῖσαν ἐκ θεῶν . . .

I have heard of one woman only, one of all those before, who has laid her hand against her dear children, Ino, who was made mad by the gods.

(1282–84)

This omission prompts Page to remark: "they might have added at least Agave and Procne" (xx, n. 8). The Agave parallel that he cites is only partial, however—as, in fact, is the Chorus's Ino parallel (see Newton)—since it was in a state of divinely inflicted delusion that Agave unwittingly slew her son. On the other hand, the Procne parallel is so close (involving murder of one's own child specifically to gain revenge on his father) as to be inescapable. In fact, Euripides has turned Medea's story into a doublet for Procne's. The Chorus's omission of this precise parallel, then, issues an invitation—rather, a challenge—to the audience to supply it. Once they do, as I shall argue below, they are further invited to note not only the similarities but also the differences between the two wives, Medea and Procne, with the result that Medea's crime seems even worse, since its provocation was so much less.

11. All that can be stated with certainty is that the *Tereus* appeared before Aristophanes' *Av.* was produced in 414. See Knox, 322 n. 80, on some scholars' suggestions. Knox himself concludes that the issue is unconcludable.

12. See above, n. 10, and text, pp. 4f. Newton concludes: "Simply stated, there are no genuine mythological examples to mitigate the horror of Medea's

actions. For Ino offers no parallel: Medea's crime, lacking a precedent, is truly ἀνήκουστον ['unheard of']" (502).

13. E.g., esp. by Bongie (Intro., n. 1). See also below, pp. 55f.

14. Grube, 148.

15. Perhaps the most unambiguous primary testimony on this question is the tale told in the *Life of Aeschylus*, that a performance of the *Eum.* induced spontaneous abortions in women in the audience. Evidence, argument, and counterargument may be reviewed in A. E. Haigh, *The Attic Theatre*[3], ed. A. W. Pickard-Cambridge (Clarendon, Oxford, 1907), 323ff.; H. D. F. Kitto, *The Greeks* (Penguin, Baltimore, 1951), 233f. (both of whom argue *for* women's attendance at the theater); and in Victor Ehrenberg, *The People of Aristophanes: A Sociology of Old Attic Comedy*, 27–28 n. 2; 201; 385 (against women's attendance). With Sarah Pomeroy, *Goddesses, Whores, Wives and Slaves: Women in Classical Antiquity* (Schocken, New York, 1975), 80, I incline to the view that women did attend theatrical performances, but a definitive answer is yet to be provided.

16. See, e.g., E. R. Dodds, ed., *Euripides, Bacchae* (Oxford University Press, London, 1960; 1st pub. 1944), xxii–xxiv, on the contemporaneous burst in popularity of the orgiastic religions, which are based on the necessity of releasing repressed tensions periodically through controlled channels.

17. Conacher, 194ff., for instance, emphasizes the mitigating effects of the onslaught of Medea's waverings. Noting the coldness of Medea's announced plan to murder her children and styling its speaker "an embodiment of the *alastōr* ['avenging spirit']," he goes on: "If this is the Medea which we are to watch without relief to the Play's end, then both the Chorus and ourselves have been the dupes, both of the 'heroine' and of the dramatist, for yielding our sympathy and interest. Fortunately, however, it is the air of cold inflexibility which is false: a cloak of desperate resolution hiding the maternal anguish as well as a device by which the dramatist may, in the end, present that anguish more effectively" (194). I do not disagree. However, as so often in Euripides, the effect is not unidirectional.

18. Cp. the related appearances of *thumos* and its cognates at 108, 271, 865, 879, 883, 1056 (discussed, pp. 56ff.), 1152.

19. It is just so that Kitto, 201–2, portrays Medea. Such a view is more commonly attributed to the goddesses Aphrodite and Artemis of Euripides' *Hipp.*

20. See Page, at 894.

21. As Page notes, at 1020: "This is very pathetic: they will not need to-day οἷα χρὴ καθ᾽ ἡμέραν ['the daily necessities'], nor ever again."

22. Page (at 809–10) notes an apt comment by Lessing: "Moral excellence in ancient Greece consisted no less in unremitting hatred of your foes than in unalterable love toward your friends." He then cites a number of parallels from lyric, choral, and tragic poetry, as well as a contrast with Plato (*Cri.* 49B). I would add that, in the context of the break-up of Jason and Medea's household, especially pertinent reference may be made to Hom. *Od.* 6.180–85, where (by contrast) Odysseus defines the functioning family unit constituted by a harmonious husband and wife as the greatest of goods and as representing πόλλ᾽ ἄλγεα δυσμενέεσσι, / χάρματα δ᾽ εὐμενέτῃσι: "a source of great grief

to their enemies, and joy to their friends" (*Od.* 6.184–85). Cp. Sophocles, *Aj.* 78–79, 382, 454ff., 956–59 et al., to *Med.* 797, 1049–52, specifically on the fear of an enemy's laughter. Knox (see esp. 297–300) adduces these sentiments along with other evidence to make an enlightening comparison between Medea and the Sophoclean hero; cp. Bongie. It should be noted, however, that these sentiments are not merely "heroic," but part of the code of the everyday 5th–4th century Athenian. In the *Cri.* excerpt cited by Page, Socrates asseverates that: οὐδὲ [δεῖ] ἀδικούμενον ἄρα ἀνταδικεῖν, ὡς οἱ πολλοὶ οἴονται: "nor [must one], when wronged, do wrong in return, *as the many think*" (emphasis mine). And Socrates' quest for a definition of justice in the *Resp.* grows largely out of a desire to refute just such popular sentiment, as expressed by Polemarchus: *Resp.* I.332C; cp. 333E.

23. Cp. Easterling, 185.
24. Bongie, 55.
25. Bongie, 56.
26. See below, 66f., 71ff. In both plays, the heroine's masculinization is a recurrent topic.
27. For opposed views of the "sacrifice," see Page, *ad loc.*, and Pucci, 133ff.; and see below, 74ff.
28. David Kovacs, "On Medea's Great Monologue," *CQ* N.S. 36:2 (1986), 343–52, argues with a measure of persuasiveness for excision of lines 1056–64. In doing so he characterizes lines 1056–58 as "high fustian" and the distinction of Medea and her *thumos* as a "frigid conceit" (348 n. 8). These aesthetic judgments seem inordinately extreme. On the other hand, athetesis of the passage does resolve other problems (the borrowing of lines 1062–63 from 1240–41 and the non-Attic passive usage of *ekpheuxetai* at 1064) and can be achieved without violence to the moving and clearly genuine lines 1065–80, which have often engendered surgical impulses in other critics. Nonetheless, I will continue to treat these lines as Euripidean as Kovacs's suggestions undergo the tests of time and critical response.
29. See citations in Page, *ad loc.*
30. Cp. Knox, 298; Schlesinger, 29–30.
31. Cp. Pucci, 138–39.
32. Collinge, 172 n. 7.
33. Page, at 1058; cp. Schlesinger, 30ff.
34. Kovacs, 343. The Reeve quotation is from M. D. Reeve, "Euripides, *Medea* 1021–1080," *CQ* N.S. 22 (1972), 51–61, which includes a full bibliography on the question. Kovacs goes on to argue for excision of only 1056–64 (see above, n. 28)—a suggestion which has certain appeal on other grounds.
35. See pp. 17ff. and Intro., n. 13.
36. Kovacs's argument (350–52) for "reinterpretation" of these lines seems unnecessary, though well motivated. I agree with his assertion (following Christman and Lloyd-Jones) that in referring to the ills brought to men by *thumos* (1080) Medea is thinking most specifically of the ill she is bringing upon herself; but I see no need, with Kovacs et al., to make a sharp distinction in line 1078 between "doing" ill and "suffering" ill (Kovacs opts for the reading *tolmēsō* over *dran mellō*): the ill the character says she is about to cause will be general, affecting her enemies (Jason, Creon, the princess), herself, and

her children (who are but innocent victims). To take the line so does not of necessity involve reading of the passage as moralistic reflection on the right or wrong of harming others; Medea merely acknowledges here (in loftier language than mine) that her *thumos* is driving her on despite her awareness of what a mess she is about to make of things.

37. See Murray (1946), 149ff., for an exemplary effort. Kitto offers a capsulized, but similarly grand generalization when he summarizes the Chorus's "truest" function as that of "conveying lyrically the tragic idea" (262). This is not to demur, but merely to emphasize that, although they obviously do play an exalting role in the dramatic overview, no one (I think) would attempt to defend a large portion of their statements of opinion as anything above the ordinary, from an intellectual or philosophical standpoint.

38. The Chorus in this play has frequently come under severe criticism from scholars, on charges ranging from irrelevance to treachery against their native city to moral paralysis in their failure to intercede on the children's behalf. They have seemed perfectly illustrative of Murray's trenchant formulation ([1946], 149): "The objections to the Chorus are plain to any infant"; cp. Murray (1906), 82–83, on the Chorus of the *Med.* specifically. By asserting that they are in some ways "reflective of 'normal' human reaction," I of course do not mean to imply that the sins regularly imputed to them constitute "normal" human failings. Rather, I take as a given that the playwright has granted the Chorus an essentially passive role in the play. Their assigned function here is to reflect on others' actions, not to act themselves. No amount of critical wishfulness will make them lift up their cudgels; it is a vain exercise for critics to judge their actions, or lack thereof, as if they were a character in the play, when the playwright has clearly shaped them not as an actor but as a sensibility. For a parallel assertion, see Easterling, 178: ". . . we accept their inactivity because these women are not at the centre of the play: they are peripheral figures whose role is not to do and suffer but to comment, sympathize, support or disapprove."

39. Cp. Conacher's tracing of the progression in the Chorus's emotions (Conacher, 188–93) and Kitto's brief notice of their turnaround, which he likens to that of the Chorus in the *Ant.* (Kitto, 260–61).

40. Whether or not one agrees with Page's excision, *ad loc.*, of line 262, after lines 374–75 the Chorus have become Medea's accomplices in her intended revenge against Creon and the princess.

41. Interestingly, though, despite the Chorus's revulsion against Medea's proposed act, they do not waver from their judgment that Jason is deserving of punishment (see lines 1231–32 and above, p. 49).

42. Norwood, 34. Kitto, 194–95, expresses much the same sentiment, though in politer terms. Another view of the ode's pertinence is offered by Pucci, 144–48.

43. I follow Murray's text in line 157, retaining the *keinōi* of the codices and punctuating after *tode*: "This is his right (sc. *parestin*); do not be angry." Page, following Verrall, emends to *koinon* ("This is common; do not be angry"). Either of these is preferable to the unpunctuated version using *keinōi*: "Do not be angry at him for this."

44. There is, perhaps, purposeful and slightly wicked irony implicit in the

Chorus's faith that Zeus will advocate for Medea against her adulterous husband. Zeus *horkios:* "protector of oaths" he may be, but he can nonetheless hardly escape his reputation as divine adulterer *par excellence.*

Chapter 4

1. The three quotations from Page appear on xv and xvii.
2. Page, xvii.
3. See above, pp. 27ff.
4. The strength of audience expectation that the two opposed parties should represent opposed values of some sort is aptly attested by Schlesinger's statement, regardless of the outcome of the play, that "Hier bei Euripides dagegen ist die Welt des Mannes vollkommen enthumanisiert . . . Ihm tritt in Medea die Frau gegenüber als Vertreterin der menschlichen Werte und Bindungen" (45).
5. *Pace* Vellacott, 106–7. Grube, however, agrees (159).
6. Burnett (1973), 9ff.
7. Burnett (1973), 7.
8. This conclusion concerning Jason runs counter to Burnett's own, since she sees Jason's characterization as unremittingly debased (see esp. 15ff.).
9. The appropriateness of Tiresias's position as second mediator is reinforced by his own mythic biography, for, somewhat like Athena, Tiresias too was androgynous, having lived, in his time, as both man and woman.
10. A parallel critical approach to that taken here is adopted by Burnett (1973), 11. In much the same way as I note Euripides' refusal to let the children function as the "mediators" which the audience might, by tradition, expect, Burnett asserts that he declined to let them play a role, traditional within revenge tragedies, as subjects of a rescue subplot (who might have been saved by their mother from early betrayal by Jason and exile by Creon). Through such rescue subplots, identified as traditional parts of the genre by Burnett, the criminality of the final act of vengeance is, typically, mitigated. Burnett notes the chaotic effect in the *Med.* of the playwright's refusal of such palliatives: "When they are given death instead of a fresh life, when their bodies and not those of the princess and her father are displayed in the tableau at the end, the lost possibility of redemption joins the hideous actuality of crime to create the momentary impression that the tragic cosmos has got out of joint, that the stage has betrayed us, and that things are far worse here than art has been licensed to show" (11).
11. Murray (1906), xi.
12. Page, *ad loc.*
13. Burkert (1966), 118–19.
14. Pucci, 135; see also ch. 1, n. 20.
15. Another mythic example of a daughter sacrificed by her father was also treated by Euripides. His *Erechtheus* tells the story of that Athenian king's sacrifice of his daughter(s) in response to an oracle that he might thus win a war with the Eleusinians (see, e.g., Apollod., *Bibl.* 3.15.4); several fragments are preserved, including two long ones (frs. 360 and 362 [Nauck]). Brief allusion is made to the story by Creusa (a surviving daughter) at *Ion* 277–80.

16. Foley, 39.
17. Foley, 38.
18. Zeitlin (1965) and (1966).
19. Euripides, of course, in the *IA*, his late play on the subject of the sacrifice of Iphigenia, perpetrates upon Agamemnon himself an extreme degeneration of motivation; at least as seen through the eyes of Menelaus, his decision to sacrifice his daughter is motivated purely by his own self-seeking political ambition, and his dramatic show of ambivalence is mere posturing.
20. See, e.g., previous discussions of the comparisons drawn implicitly between Medea and Procne and explicitly between Medea and Ino; of Medea's assertion of her communality with the Greek Everywoman; of the suggestion that this play's conflict between husband and wife will fall into the mold exemplified by that between Agamemnon and Clytemnestra as representatives respectively of state and family; and of the initial expectation that this play, like the *Oresteia*, will admit of some eventual mediation of the conflicts played out onstage.
21. On the motif of virgin sacrifice, see, e.g., Foley, 65ff.
22. Conacher, 190 n. 11.

Chapter 5

1. See above, pp. 26ff. For elaboration of the child-parent obligation, see A. Lumpe, "Eltern," *RAC* IV (1959), cols. 1191–94. A significant entry in the vocabulary of *trophē* is the verb *stergō*: "love," which was especially used of the mutual affection between parent and child (see LSJ I.1); cp. *Med.* 88, where Jason's failure to love (*stergein*) his children is contrasted pointedly by the *Paidagōgos* with his sexual connection with the princess (*eunēs*).
2. Beyond this passage from the *Supp.* and those to be cited from the *Med.*, see, e.g., the passages cited on pp. 87–89 below; *Alc.* 662–68; *Tro.* 1180–88; *Ion* 109–11, 136–37, 318ff., et al.
3. Page, at 1334, asserts that the fact that the murder is committed *parestion* aligns Euripides' version with that cited by the Scholiast to Apollonius 4.228 rather than with the dismemberment motif (Pherecyd., *Fr. Gr. Hist.* 3F326 Jac.)—that grisly reworking of the folk topic represented by the tale of Atalanta and the golden apples by which Medea chops her young brother into pieces and scatters him bit by bit across the sea to slow her father's pursuit. It is true that Euripides remains silent about dismemberment. However, the tradition which is distinctly barred by the epithet *parestion* is the one followed by Apollonius, in which an adult Apsyrtus pursues Jason and Medea and is murdered by Jason during an assignation on an island (Ap. Rhod. 4.410ff.). Finally, I have wondered if Jason's final words in the play (his lament that Medea has precluded him from a father's appointed role in his children's burial [1408–14]) may have called to others' minds, as to my own, her earlier implication in a burial issue: in the form of the myth in which the dismemberment figures, it is in order to perform his parental duty of burying the scattered pieces of his son's body that Aeetes lets Medea escape his pursuit.
4. It is somewhat unclear from the mythic sources how old an element in

the saga the princess is (see Page, xxvff.) and (if old) what the nature of her role in the story was before Euripides; but, whatever degree of innovation may have been used by Euripides here, it is clear that he has chosen to emphasize the father-daughter relationship between Creon and the princess for his own dramatic and thematic purposes.

5. On *paida basileōs*, cp. the princess's initial characterization in the play (as early as line 19) as *Kreontos paid'*. It may not be too fanciful to relate the princess's namelessness in the play to the playwright's effort to emphasize her role in a significant parent-child relationship.

6. There is a specific echo of this line, as well as of Creon's cry οἴμοι, συνθάνοιμί σοι, τέκνον: "Alas, may I die along with you, my child!" (1210), in Euripides' own *Hec.*, when Hecuba announces to Odysseus her intention to die along with the soon-to-be-sacrificed Polyxena: πολλή γ' ἀνάγκη θυγατρὶ συνθανεῖν ἐμέ./ . . . / ὁποῖα κισσὸς δρυός, ὅπως τῆσδ' ἕξομαι: "I must altogether die with my daughter . . . I shall cling to her like ivy to an oak" (*Hec.* 396–98). In this example, as in the *Med.*, it is love of parent and child which is at question (though the *Hec.* passage lacks the wry twist contained in the destructive clinging of Creusa to Creon). For the trope used of a lover's embrace see Eubulus, fr. 104.1ff.K.; Catull. 61.33–35, 106–9; Hor. *Carm.* 1.36.18–20, *Epod.* 15.5–6; Gall. *Epithal.* 3 (*Anth. Lat.* 232 Mey.); Stat. *Silv.* 5.1.48ff.; Claud. 14.18ff.; Paul. Sil. *Anth. Pal.* 5.255.13ff.; cp. Ov. *Met.* 14.661–68.

7. See 1130; cp. 1298, where by metonymy Creon's house (*dōmata*) is seen as the would-be means of Corinthian vengeance against Medea. It is perhaps also notable that in death the princess leaves her father's home for the house of Hades (. . . ἥτις εἰς ῞Αιδου δόμους / οἴχῃ γάμων ἕκατι τῶν Ἰάσονος: "who for the sake of her marriage to Jason is gone to the house (*domous*) of Hades" [1234–35]; this inverted allusion to a bride's normal departure from her father's home upon marriage ("marriage to Hades" was a common Greek trope for a pubescent girl's premature death) is pointedly paralleled to Medea's own departure from her childhood abode, also for the sake of marriage to Jason:

. . . οὔτε μοι πατρὶς
οὔτ' οἶκος ἔστιν οὔτ' ἀποστροφὴ κακῶν.
ἡμάρτανον τόθ' ἡνίκ' ἐξελίμπανον
δόμους πατρῴους, ἀνδρὸς ῞Ελληνος λόγοις
πεισθεῖσ'. . .

As for me, I have not fatherland, nor home, nor refuge from ills. Truly I erred when I left my father's home, persuaded by the words of a Greek husband . . .

(798–802)

8. Note the parallel construction of these lines and *Supp.* 363 (quoted above, p. 82): i.e., a description of child-parent *trophē*, followed by a summary appositive phrase (*zelōton anthrōpoisi*: "enviable lot among men" :: *kalliston eranon*: "loveliest loan"); note also the appearance in both passages of the epithet *dustēnos*: "wretched" for the person who fails of *trophē*.

9. While the topicality of the Aegeus-episode to an Athenian audience is patent, dramatically the scene has come under a great deal of criticism. Although Page in an edition first published in 1938 used the past tense of such blame-laying ("The scene in which Aegeus appears before Medea used to be

severely criticized" [xxix]), the scene even currently stands arraigned in the 1970 edition of the *OCD* as a "blemish" (Lucas, 420). The prejudice begins with Aristotle: the scene is presumed to offend against his law of necessary sequence (*Poet*. 9.1451^b. 33–35). The problem is summed up pithily and picturesquely by Kitto (198): ". . . Aegeus comes out of the blue, like a railway accident." Euripides is frequently defended against this "tedious" criticism (as Conacher [190] calls it), but it seems to have been impossible to lay it to its final rest. To cite only a few examples of the scene's recent defense: Buttrey, 5–10, demonstrates its structurally pivotal position in the play, both formally and emotionally; Easterling, 184–85, adds some notable points, as does J. Roger Dunkle, "The Aegeus Episode," *TAPA* 100 (1969), 97–107; Browne, 76–77, suggests that lines 674–77 hint that Aegeus had purposely sought Medea out as a *sophē*: "wise woman" who might solve the oracle's riddle (as he does in Neophron's version of the play [see Schol. 666; fr. 1 (Nauck)]). Also pertinent may be a set of observations made in a different context by Burnett (1971), 30. In describing the "rescue piece" (a recurrent mode in Euripides' plays), Burnett says that this form "presupposes a victim immobilized and in danger from a threatening creature; . . . after a prologue of lament, the normal stage action begins with the arrival (*properly accidental* [emphasis mine]) of the hero. . . . The proper ending of the play is some form of translation . . . often associated with marriage." If we accept Burnett's formulation as a correct delineation of the elements of the form, then apply it to the *Med*., difficulties with the Aegeus-episode become soluble. Before Aegeus's arrival, Medea is "immobilized" in her plan for revenge because she has nowhere to turn for refuge once the crime is committed (see lines 386–91); the wrath of the Corinthians represents the threat she faces. Her plight is resolved by the "properly accidental" arrival of Aegeus. The play ends with Medea's "translation," via magic chariot, to Athens, where mythic tradition informs us she undertakes to live in marriage with Aegeus.

10. Euripides himself told the story of Medea at Athens in his *Aeg*. (date unknown). If the *Aeg*. actually predated the *Med*., as many have posited, following Wilamowitz, Euripides' own version of the later doings of Medea would inform the audience's forecast of trouble to come for Aegeus. If the *Aeg*. was produced after the *Med*. (see Knox, *W. & A.*, 295 and 316 n. 5, for dispute of the presumption of an early date), the evidence of vase-paintings depicting the story of Medea, Aegeus, and Theseus, dating from the mid-fifth century on, indicate at least that the story was part of received myth by that time; it may therefore be reasonably inferred that the audience of 431 B.C. was familiar with its outlines.

Chapter 6

1. A partial analogy for the metaphorical identification of country and family may be found in the more primitive anthropomorphizing explication of the cosmos in terms of family relations (e.g., in the Hesiodic picture of Earth/ *Gē* as wife of Sky/*Ouranos* and mother to all that comes thereafter). However, the explication of country in terms of family is a great deal more complex. The concept of *mētropolis*: "mother city" includes both the simple sense of "the

land we live in," the land which affords us food, shelter, and other necessities of life, and the more abstract sense of "the state," through which individuals bind themselves by common laws and principles to live and work in common. In the former sense, the metaphorical identification of the country with the family is clearly born of their similarities as nurturers. In the latter, however, it is motivated by both similarities (the properly symbiotic relationship between parent and child) and dissimilarities. The potential for conflict between family and state is a theme regularly treated by Greek myth and literature (e.g., throughout the Agamemnon cycle, most notably in the *Eum.*; and in the *Ant.*). Thus, the explication of the allegiance the citizen owes to the state by analogy to proper familial order necessarily involves a didactic element, adjuring the citizen to the same sense of responsibility as he/she accepts as family member, and (as well) an element of legitimation of an artificial societal order (the state) by the metaphorical assumption of terms adopted from the realm of a more "natural" societal unit (the family).

2. James Daly, "*Oedipus Coloneus*: Sophocles' *Threpteria* to Athens. I," *Quaderni Urbinati di Cultura Classica* N.S. 22:1 (1986), 75–93. In brief, Oedipus is seen on the family level in dichotomized relation to his two sets of children: on the one hand, his sons, who pursue their own internecine squabble in self-interested disregard of their father's plight, and, on the other, his daughters (especially Antigone), who piously provide the support for Oedipus's infirm old age which is required by the reciprocal system of *trophē*. Interwoven with this theme is the related contrast between two cities and two kings: Thebes, with its callous and opportunistic king Creon, attempts to elicit benefit from its expatriate citizen Oedipus after having deprived him, through his exile, of the *trophē* expected from a mother city; Athens, ruled by the ideally virtuous and proto-democratic Theseus, on the other hand, graciously receives the wandering outcast and so will reap for itself the benison of his translation and cult.

3. Both these mentions of Medea's violations of "hearths," in turn, invest Medea's earlier prayer that Aegeus admit her to his hearth with similarly ominous significance: δέξαι δὲ χώρᾳ καὶ δόμοις ἐφέστιον: "Receive me in your land at the hearth of your home" (713); cp. 681.

4. D. W. Lucas, *OCD*, 2nd ed. (Oxford University Press, London, 1970), *s.v.* "Euripides," 420. Page (viii) goes one step further, to conjecture that, since the *Med.* was produced in the spring just preceding the outbreak of the Peloponnesian War, "this is the last hour in which the making of this ode was possible." The pathos of this assertion, however, is belied by the fact that over twenty years later Sophocles, in his *OC*, could describe Athens's virtues— both topographical and moral—in terms equally glowing; see esp. the chorus at *OC* 668ff. Page's succeeding argument that Euripides' artistry made him a "partner" in Athens's decline (viii), and that "it was the worse for Athens" that he wrote as he did (ix), would have recommended itself to the Socrates of *Resp.* 10.

5. Cp. Euripides, *Heracl.* (Demophon), *Supp.* (Theseus); partial prototypes exist in Aeschylus, *Eum.* (with Athena in the "king's" role), *Supp.* (same motif, but set in Argos).

6. Page, xxv. For further discussion, see above, pp. 00ff. Even if one assumes that the deliberate child-murder was an original element in the

Medea-saga, the problem remains, for (given the political temper of his times) even to have chosen this version from among other variants could have been viewed as pro-Corinthian.

7. Cp. Vellacott, 25; Herbert Musurillo, "Euripides' *Medea:* A Reconsideration," *AJP* 87 (1966), 59 ("The Attic king stands as a vivid contrast to the autocratic, bumbling Creon of Corinth"); Page, xiii; G. M. A. Grube, *The Drama of Euripides* (London, 1941), 152; Dunkle, 105–6.

8. Dunkle, 98ff., argues that Medea and Aegeus are equally motivated by self-interest and so equally tarnished. While I agree with much of Dunkle's presentation of a theme of self-interest in the play, Aegeus's fallibility in this regard seems mild compared with Medea's and Jason's. Aegeus is characterized as an amiable old gent. Even if there may be an element of opportunism in his accession to Medea's request for protection, there is no manipulativeness on his part, merely a happy coincidence of his interest with that of the person he is called upon to help; set in disjunction against Jason, whose feeble self-justifications convict him of the ingratitude he denies, Aegeus is a paragon; set against Medea, he is proved the rankest amateur in the game of self-service.

9. Cp. Knox, 300–301; Murray (1906), 91.

10. F. A. Paley, ed., *Euripides, With an English Commentary*, vol. I (Whittaker, London, 1857), 70.

11. Page, xix.

12. It might be objected that Creon had other children to carry on his line, since plurals are used of his progeny at lines 329 and 344. As Euripides tells the tale, however, it seems that the kingship of Corinth will pass to Jason upon his matrilocal marriage with the princess (see esp. 916–17, in which Jason foresees his and Medea's sons' assumption of a leading role in Corinth as a result of their kinship with the sons to be born of him and Creusa). Presented with this presumption concerning accession, we may be justified in concluding at least that Creon had no handy male heir.

13. Conacher fully appreciates the Chorus's expression here of "the hideous uncongeniality between Medea the child-murderer and the pure and serene haven which she has chosen" (193). Focusing on Medea, he sees the contrast as a purposeful expression of the "self-destruction which her plans involve." He does not, however, go one step further, to switch focus to the other half of the comparison and comment on the destructive effects of that uncongeniality on the city which must absorb Medea's pollution. He thus leaves unqualified his earlier inference of essentially patriotic authorial intent in the still uncomplicated first strophe and antistrophe: "Euripides may well have enjoyed pleasing his fellow citizens and himself with such idealized pictures of his city" (192). Burnett (1973), 23–24, *does* examine the implications of Medea's entry into Athens but comes to an almost opposite conclusion from mine; she sees in the city's serene ability to "digest one more demon of punishment" and in Aegeus's fidelity to his oaths an ultimate redemption of the corruption of the play's events.

14. Daly, 75–76 n. 2. He elaborates: "Aesch. *Cho.* 6 shows Orestes dedicating to Inachus a πλόκαμον . . . θρεπτήριον as a thank-offering for his upbringing. The Greeks of course considered rivers to be κουροτρόφοι (cf. Hes. *Th.* 346–348); hence, upon reaching manhood, young boys were accustomed to

offer a shorn lock of hair to their country's rivers, in order to repay the debt for nurture owed to them (*Il.* XXIII 138–151 contain the earliest and best known reference to this ritual)."

Conclusion

1. My assertion that an implicit comparison between the dramatic world of the *Med.* and Hesiod's fifth and worst age is suggested by the protagonist's breach of *trophē* is lent support by Burnett (1973). She notes (20) a further identification of the moral chaos of the *Med.* with that of Hesiod's Iron Age, as embodied in lost respect for oaths: on *Med.* 439 (ὅϱκων χάϱις: "the grace of oaths"), cp. *Op.* 190; on *Med.* 439–40 (οὐδ' ἔτ' αἰδὼς / Ἑλλάδι τᾷ μεγάλᾳ μένει: "no shame remains in great Greece"), cp. *Op.* 197–200.

2. Murray (1906), 53.

3. *Alc.*, *Hel.*, *Andr.*, *Bacch.* The first line of the epilogue in the *Med.* is different from the others, which begin: πολλαὶ μοϱφαὶ τῶν δαιμονίων: "the ways of god have many forms."

4. In my translation, I have taken the aorists *etelesthē* and *hēure* not as gnomic aorists, but as true aorists, moving the statement from the gnomic sentiment voiced in its first two lines (and placed there in the more normal gnomic tense, the present) into the realm of the particularized occurrences of this play, thus aligning 1417–18 more closely with 1419 ("So has gone this affair") than with the generalized truths of 1415–16.

5. A detailed discussion of such "tail-pieces" occurs in W. S. Barrett, ed., *Euripides: Hippolytos* (Oxford University Press, Oxford, 1964), at 1462–66. Barrett voices general suspicion of Euripidean tail-pieces, proceeding from two cases of repetition from one play to another, of which this is the more extreme. He concludes that, if the lines were genuinely by Euripides, they were composed for the *Alc.* alone and in the other four cases were "added later to cater for a public addicted to sententious commonplaces." It is possible that he is correct in his conclusion, but I would challenge the premises from which he arrives at it. In discussing this particular epilogue, Barrett says, for instance: "Now Eur. if any man was an adept moralizer, and it would be extraordinary that he should content himself in almost one play in three with a repetition of the same undistinguished platitude; suspicion deepens when one observes that only in *Al.* is the platitude really appropriate—in *An.*, *Hel.*, and *Ba.* it is no more than tolerable and in *Med.* it is grossly out of place." Our first point of disagreement is immediately apparent, since I will assert here that the lines are highly appropriate to the very play where he sees them as most egregiously anomalous. Second, the above quotation makes it clear that underlying Barrett's suspiciousness of the epilogue is a general aesthetic demand for variation and originality—a demand which is innate to the modern critic but perhaps should not be readily attached to the ancient artisan. Further, while it is true that Euripides can at times assume the posture of an "adept moralizer," it is equally true (and characteristic of his art) that he can quite intently *decline* to point a moral. In fact, this little epilogue on the achievement of the unexpected provides him with a handy means of shifting the ground from the moral questions the audience would *like* to see answered

to a comment which characterizes not only the vicissitudes of life but also the refusal of his artistic technique to stay within the bounds of the expected. And, finally, Barrett's unelaborated presumption that repetition of an epilogue from one play to another, while "extraordinary" in a playwright, would be natural from an actor is not compelling. An equally persuasive inference would be that an actor might demand a tail-piece which exhibited stricter relevance to the plot, while Euripides could find congenial the adoption of a generalized and formulaic closing of this sort, for the artistic purposes outlined above.

   6. Whitman, v; cp. Buttrey, 17.

   7. C. Collard, *Euripides* (*Greece and Rome: New Surveys in the Classics* 14, Oxford University Press, Oxford, 1981), 32–33 and nn. 13–14 to those pages, cites (with abundant bibliographical reference) trends and excesses in interpretation of political allusions in Euripides; Collard's own formulation of the balanced critical perspective on such allusions is well conceived: "So lively was Euripides' interest in the totality of Athens' life, that he brought his *polis* into the mythic world more obviously and consistently than Sophocles and even Aeschylus. . . . The special problem in Euripides is to measure the productive tensions thus created, as present microcosm and timeless macrocosm illuminate each other" (32).

   8. Pucci, 17.

   9. *Ibid.* See also 166: ". . . failure is unavoidable. Confusion instead of understanding, excess instead of discriminating details, ambivalence and contiguity instead of distinctions, overlapping instead of paradox, polysemy instead of transparency, violence instead of harmony—all threaten Euripides' goal at each moment."

Glossary

Aeetes. King of the Colchians; father of Medea. He sets an "impossible" task for Jason upon the Argonauts' arrival in Colchis: he must yoke fire-breathing bulls and sow a field with dragon's teeth; these sprout into warriors, who must in turn be slain. Aided by an infatuated Medea, Jason accomplishes the impossible and flees with Medea and the Golden Fleece.

Aegeus. King of Athens; consults the oracle at Delphi concerning his childlessness and is told in ambiguous language to remain sexually continent until he arrives home; failing to understand the oracle, he begets Theseus by Aethra, daughter of his host, Pittheus of Troezen. He offers refuge to Medea after her Corinthian exploits; by some accounts they have a son, Medus. He expels Medea from Athens after she tries to poison Theseus before his recognition by his father.

Agamemnon. King of Argos; son of Atreus, brother of Menelaus, husband of Clytemnestra. In order to lead the Greek expedition to Troy, he sacrifices his daughter Iphigenia to the goddess Artemis, thus angering Clytemnestra, who joins with her lover (Agamemnon's cousin) Aegisthus to kill him upon his return to Argos.

anagnōrisis. "Recognition"; in tragedy, a conventional climactic element of plot which leads to dénouement.

anangkē. "Force," "constraint," "necessity," "compulsion"; as opposed to free will.

anomia. "Lawlessness," "negation of law." Etymologically: from **a-** ("without") + **nomos** ("custom," "law," "custom-law": that which *should* be done because it always *has* been done).

apaidia. "Childlessness."

apais. "Childless."

apolis. "Without city, state, or country"; "banished," "outlaw."

aporia. "Difficulty," "perplexity," "state of being at a loss."

Apsyrtus. Brother of Medea; in alternate versions of the myth, he is (a) a child taken by Medea when she flees Colchis; she kills him, cuts his body into pieces, then throws one piece at a time overboard to deter her father's pursuit (like Atalanta with the golden apples, Aeetes must stop repeatedly to pick up pieces and so cannot catch the fugitives); or (b) an adult who leads the chase on behalf of his father (as in Ap. Rhod.) and is killed after an assignation by Jason.

aretē. "Goodness," "excellence"; the area of enterprise within which a person is or should be skilled.

charis. "Grace," "favor," "beauty"; concretely, "favor," "boon."

Circe. Daughter of Helios, sister of Aeetes; demigoddess who dwells on the island of Aeaea; in Homer she uses her magical powers to turn Odysseus's men into swine but later becomes enamored of Odysseus and helps him on his journey (after a year's dalliance).

Clytemnestra. Daughter of Tyndareus, sister of Helen, wife of Agamemnon; her vengeance on her husband, originally motivated by his sacrifice of their daughter Iphigenia, provides the subject matter for Aeschylus's trilogy (*Agamemnon, Choephori, Eumenides*) and, with its aftermath, for Sophocles' *Electra* and Euripides' *Electra, Iphigenia Aulidensis, Iphigenia Taurica,* and *Orestes.* Especially as presented in the *Eumenides* in alliance with the Furies, she is seen as a traditional champion of family allegiance over state allegiance.

Creon. = Gk. Κρέων ("ruling one," "king"); as such, a stock name attached to several figures in myth, including (a) the king of Corinth in Euripides' account of Medea's Corinthian exploits, killed by Medea in the course of the play; and (b) Iocasta's brother, Oedipus's brother-in-law; king or regent of Thebes who after the attack of the Seven against Thebes decrees that Polyneices should receive no honor of burial; this decree brings him into conflict with Antigone, Oedipus's daughter and Polyneices' sister, whose burial of Polyneices and subsequent martyrdom provide the subject matter of Sophocles' *Antigone.*

Creusa. = Gk. Κρέουσα (the feminine form of Κρέων: "ruling woman," i.e., "princess"), and as such a stock name applied to several figures in myth, among them (a) the daughter of the Athenian king Erechtheus whose violation by Apollo sets the stage for Euripides' *Ion;* and (b) the princess, daughter of Creon of Corinth, who weds Jason and so brings Medea's murderous wrath upon herself and her father; this character remains unnamed throughout Euripides' play but is alternatively attributed this name and the name Glauce by later sources.

daimōn. "God," "divinity"; as it denotes the metaphysical power which controls people's destiny, it also comes to mean "fate" or "destiny," or simply one's "lot" or "fortune."

domos. "House," "household," "family."

echthros (pl. -oi). "Enemy"; as opposed to **philos** (pl. -oi).

eidos (pl. -ea). "Form," "idea," "ideal form," "archetype"; in Platonic philosophy, the **eidea** (= **ideai**) are the ideal and perfect forms of things; they are absolute and appreciable only by the intellect.

ektrephō. "Rear," "raise from childhood"; cognate with **trophē**; see also **exethrepsamēn.**

eukosmia. "Orderly behavior," "good conduct."

exethrepsamēn. From **ektrephō,** first-person aorist middle form: "I reared [for myself]," "I raised from childhood [for myself]."

gaia = **gē.** "Earth," "land," "country." Personified, "Earth" is a semi-anthropomorphized female deity who weds her child Οὐρανός: Uranus ("Sky," "Heaven") and becomes mother both of various topographical entities (seas, mountains) and of the Titans from whom the Olympian gods are descended.

gēroboskēsein. Future infinitive of **gēroboskeō:** "to feed or cherish in old age"; a term applied especially to one's parents and a significant item in the vocabulary of **trophē.**

Glauce. Alternative name applied by later sources to the Corinthian princess killed by Medea in Euripides' play; see also **Creusa.**

gunē en gunaixin. "Woman among women."

Haemon. In Sophocles' *Antigone,* Creon's son and Antigone's fiancé, who tries to act as mediator between Creon and Antigone; he commits suicide when he finds Antigone dead.

Iphigenia. Daughter of Agamemnon and Clytemnestra; older sister of Electra and Orestes; lured with her mother to Aulis on promise of marriage to Achilles, she is sacrificed to Artemis by her father so the contrary winds which have bound the fleet may cease and the Greek army's departure for Troy may be expedited; in some versions (the *Cypria,* followed, e.g., by Euripides, *Iphigenia Taurica*), a hind is substituted for the girl in the moment just before the sacrifice, and she is sequestered in the country of the Taurians until rescued and returned home by Orestes.

kai ta dokēthent' ouk etelesthē. "What was expected was not brought to fulfillment" = *Med.* 1417, from the play's epilogue.

kardia. "Heart," especially as the locus for emotions.

mētropolis. "Mother city," "mother country," "home."

nomoi brotōn. "Laws of mankind," "ways of mortals"; see *Medea* 812.

oikos. "House," "reigning house," "family"; in Attic law, "inheritance," "estate"; the duty to propagate children was a critical component of the social duty to preserve and perpetuate one's **oikos.**

paidagōgos. The slave who accompanied a boy to and from school and ministered to his daily needs; like the "Nurse," a stock character in drama.

pathei mathos. "Learning through suffering."

pathos (pl. **-ē**). "Experience," "suffering," "misfortune."

Peliades. The daughters of Pelias; after viewing a demonstration rejuvenation by Medea, they determine to restore their father to youth by subjecting him to a similar process (involving dismemberment and boiling in Medea's magical potion); unfortunately, Medea omits the potent herbs, rendering Pelias's daughters guilty of their father's murder; the incident is the cause of Medea and Jason's exile to Corinth. Euripides wrote a play entitled *Peliades.*

Pelias. Jason's uncle, usurper of his father's rightful throne; he sends Jason in quest of the Golden Fleece to deter his effort to reclaim the throne; upon Jason's return, Pelias's death is engineered by Medea (see **Peliades**).

peripeteia. "Turning right around," "sudden change," "reversal [of circumstances or fortunes]."

philia. "Friendship," "affection."

philos (pl. -oi). As adjective, "dear," "beloved." As substantive, "friends" (as opposed to **echthroi**), "allies," "kith and kin"; neuter superlative, **ta philtata** = one's "nearest and dearest," "dear ones" (especially of wife and children).

phonos akousios. "Involuntary/accidental killing."

poluaikos logos. "Much-rushing tale" = "widespread tale" (Page), or "impetuous tale" (*LSJ*); the word appears only here in Greek [= a *hapax legomenon*]; see ch. 1, n. 14.

pseudorkos. "False to one's oath," "perjured," "foresworn."

sōphrosunē. "Moderation," "discretion," "temperance"; a term expressive of the philosophical stance frequently espoused in tragedy (especially by the chorus or nonheroic characters like the Nurse or the *paidagōgos*), i.e., that it is most prudent to seek a modest and unassuming course of life which, as it declines to strive for the heights, so also avoids the depths; to do otherwise is to court disaster by provoking the jealousy of gods or fortune.

teknophonos. "Child-murdering."

themis. "Law (as established by custom)," "justice," "right."

thumos. "Soul," "spirit"; the seat of anger or other emotions; "heart"; hence (of the emotion itself) = "anger"; the seat of thought, "mind."

τοιόνδ᾽ ἀπέβη τόδε πρᾶγμα. = *Med.* 1419 (the last line of the play): "So has gone this affair"; on the possible iconic significance of the epilogue, see text, pp. 111ff.

trephein. Present infinitive of **trephō**: "to nurture," "to cause to grow or increase," "to rear."

trophē. "Nurture," "rearing," "sustenance."

xeinapatēs. "One who betrays/cheats a *xenos* ['host,' 'guest,' 'stranger']"; as adjective, "deceitful to a *xenos*."

xenia. "Hospitality shown to a guest"; "guest-friendship"; a sacred relationship entered into by two parties ("host" and "guest": the denotation of both by the same word [*xenos*] emphasizes the reciprocity of the relationship); through the exchange of gifts of guest-friendship, an alliance is sealed which brings the guest into a quasi-familial relation with the host, extending the protection to be gained from family members to the person who travels beyond the boundaries of his home city.

Index of Passages

Subject Index

oaths, Aegeus and, 102–3, 139 n. 13
  Jason and, 29–30, 48, 61, 104, 125 n. 7
Odysseus, 77, 109–10, 131 n. 22, 136 n. 6
Odyssey. See also Index of Passages
Oedipus, 103, 121 n. 3, 128 n. 27, 138 n. 2
Oedipus Coloneus, 95, 99, 138 n. 2. *See also*
  Index of Passages
Oresteia, 2, 7–8, 75, 109, 135 n. 20
Orestes, 17, 71, 73, 88, 120 n. 1, 121 n. 3,
  139 n. 14
Orestes, 3, 120 n. 1, 128 n. 27. *See also* In-
  dex of Passages
orgiastic religions, 131 n. 16
Ouranos (Sky), 137 n. 1

paidagogos, 124 n. 31
  of *Medea*, 35–36, 38, 48, 53, 67, 113
Parmeniscus, 10, 13, 116
Pasiphae, 129 n. 5
patrio-political criticism, 117, 141 n. 7
patriotism, 32, 71, 98–106, 115–18, 138 n.
  4, 139 n. 13
Pausanias, 10, 34
Peliades, 126 n. 16
Pelias, 33, 47, 105, 126 n. 23
  in *trophe* theme, 83–84, 89, 96, 107, 108
Peloponnesian War, 1, 3, 116–17, 138 n. 4
Pentheus, 30, 128 n. 27
Pericles, citizenship law of, 130 n. 8
Phaedra, 30, 59
philia, maternal, 5, 26, 27–29, 30
  Medea and, 30–31, 38, 40, 51–52,
    55–56, 77, 108, 113
  parental, 26–27, 107, 124 n. 4
    Agamemnon and, 88
    Chorus and, 62–63, 69
    Creon and, 38, 84–89. *See also* Creon,
      as father
    Jason and, 35–36, 38, 48, 67, 70, 113
    Medea's scorn for, 81–93, 108
    Peliades and, 83–84
  paternal, secondary to maternal, 28–29
  See also trophe, familial; *trophe*, as soci-
    etal system; women, role of, in
    fifth-century Athens
Pindar, 10, 31
Pittheus, 91, 92
plagiarism, charge of, against Euripides,
  21

Plato, 131–32 n. 22
Poetics, 137 n. 9. *See also* Index of Passages
Polemarchus, 132 n. 22
polis. *See* Chorus (of *Medea*), in civic
  theme; male-female opposition,
  family-state antinomy and; *trophe*,
  civic
politico-dynastic marriage, 47, 67
Polyphemus, 109–11
Polyxena, 78, 136 n. 6
princess (Corinthian). *See* Creusa
Procne, 32, 47–48, 130 n. 10, 135 n. 20
prologue, 4, 128 n. 27
  of *Medea*, 6, 33–35, 44

Republic, 132 n. 22, 138 n. 4
revenge plot, 69–70, 79, 115, 134 n. 10

sacrifice, in *Erechtheus*, 134 n. 15
  metaphor of, in *Medea*, 14, 16, 17, 74–
    78, 79, 115, 122–23 n. 21
  tragedy and, 12, 14–17, 75–76, 122 nn.
    15, 21
  See also Hera Acraea, cult of
Semonides, 7, 79
Socrates, 132 n. 22, 138 n. 4
Sophocles, 22, 121 n. 3, 128 n. 27, 141 n. 7
  Ajax, 119 n. 1, 132 n. 22
  Antigone, 99, 100, 133 n. 39
    male-female opposition in, 1, 8, 66,
      71, 72–73, 109, 138 n. 1
  Oedipus Coloneus, 95, 99, 138 nn. 2, 4
  Tereus, 47–48, 130 n. 11
  See also Index of Passages
sophrosune (moderation), 71
state (*polis*). *See* Chorus (of *Medea*), in civic
  theme; male-female opposition,
  family-state antinomy and; *trophe*,
  civic; *trophe*, as societal system
Suda, 21, 22. *See also* Index of Passages
Supplices (Aeschylus), 138 n. 5
Supplices (Euripides), 138 n. 5. *See also* Index of Passages
suspense, 6–7, 32–33, 37, 38, 41–42, 52,
  108–9, 127 n. 24

Telemachus, 28
Tereus, 47